READING FOR TODAY
CONCEPTS 4

FOURTH EDITION

LORRAINE C. SMITH
AND
NANCY NICI MARE

English Language Institute

Queens College

The City University of New York

NATIONAL GEOGRAPHIC
LEARNING

Australia · Brazil · Mexico · Singapore · United Kingdom · United States

NATIONAL GEOGRAPHIC
L E A R N I N G

Reading for Today 4: Concepts
Fourth Edition
Lorraine C. Smith and Nancy Nici Mare

Publisher: Sherrise Roehr

Executive Editor: Laura Le Dréan

Managing Editor: Jennifer Monaghan

Senior Development Editor:
Mary Whittemore

Editorial Assistant: Jennifer Williams-Rapa

Director of Marketing: Ian Martin

Executive Marketing Manager: Ben Rivera

Product Marketing Manager: Dalia Bravo

Senior Director, Production:
Michael Burggren

Content Production Manager:
Mark Rzeszutek

Senior Print Buyer: Mary Beth Hennebury

Compositor: Cenveo® Publisher Services

Cover and Interior Design:
Brenda Carmichael

Cover Photo: Buildings viewed from low angle.
Canary Islands, Spain. Photographer: sah.
© sah/Corbis.

For product information and technology assistance, contact us at
Cengage Learning Customer & Sales Support, cengage.com/contact

For permission to use material from this text or product,
submit all requests online at **cengage.com/permissions**
Further permissions questions can be emailed to
permissionrequest@cengage.com

ISBN: 978-1-305-57999-6

National Geographic Learning
20 Channel Center Street
Boston, MA 02210
USA

National Geographic Learning, a Cengage Learning Company, has a mission to bring the world to the classroom and the classroom to life. With our English language programs, students learn about their world by experiencing it. Through our partnerships with National Geographic and TED Talks, they develop the language and skills they need to be successful global citizens and leaders.

Locate your local office at **international.cengage.com/region**

Visit National Geographic Learning online at **NGL.Cengage.com/ELT**
Visit our corporate website at **www.cengage.com**

Printed in Mexico
Print Number: 05   Print Year: 2021

CONTENTS

SCOPE & SEQUENCE

Unit & Theme	Chapter & Title	Reading Skills	Vocabulary Skills	Critical Thinking Skills
UNIT 1 **Living in Society** Page 2	**CHAPTER 1** Learning through Video Games: Fact or Fiction Page 4	Previewing a reading Recalling information Scanning for information Summarizing information **Reading Skill Focus:** Understanding charts	Understanding meaning from context **Word Forms:** Recognizing the suffix -al Identifying parts of speech: nouns and adjectives Understanding antonyms	Describing an idea for a game Identifying and explaining reasons Evaluating the benefits of video games Assessing the author's bias
	CHAPTER 2 The Birth-Order Myth Page 22	Previewing a reading Recalling information Scanning for information Summarizing information **Reading Skill Focus:** Using headings to create an outline	Understanding meaning from context **Word Forms:** Understanding word forms: nouns and adjectives Recognizing the suffixes -ance and -ence Choosing the correct dictionary definition	Analyzing survey results Explaining opinions Discussing theories Explaining the author's tone
	CHAPTER 3 Highs and Lows in Self-Esteem Page 40	Previewing a reading Recalling information Scanning for information Summarizing information **Reading Skill Focus:** Creating a flowchart	Understanding meaning from context **Word Forms:** Understanding word forms: nouns and verbs Recognizing the suffixes -tion and -ion Understanding synonyms	Discussing self-esteem in adolescence and old age Making analogies to describe your own stages of self-esteem Inferring the author's opinion
UNIT 2 **Health and Wellness** Page 58	**CHAPTER 4** Sugar: A Not-So-Sweet Story Page 60	Previewing a reading Recalling information Scanning for information Summarizing information **Reading Skill Focus:** Understanding a timeline	Understanding meaning from context **Word Forms:** Identifying parts of speech: nouns and verbs Understanding phrasal verbs	Describing reasons Explaining answers Researching and preparing a presentation Determining the author's viewpoint

SCOPE & SEQUENCE

Unit & Theme	Chapter & Title	Reading Skills	Vocabulary Skills	Critical Thinking Skills
	CHAPTER 5 Laughter Is the Best Medicine for Your Heart—Or Is It? Page 76	Previewing a reading Scanning for information Recalling information Summarizing information **Reading Skill Focus:** Organizing information in a chart	Understanding meaning from context **Word Forms:** Recognizing the suffix -ity Understanding phrasal verbs	Discussing and comparing reasons Taking and discussing a class survey Inferring the author's viewpoint on others' opinions
	CHAPTER 6 Traditional Medicine: A Non-Western Approach to Healing Page 92	Previewing a reading Scanning for information Recalling information Summarizing information **Reading Skill Focus:** Using a Venn diagram	Understanding meaning from context **Word Forms:** Recognizing the suffix -al Choosing the correct dictionary definition	Discussing and comparing reasons Giving examples to support answers Explaining the author's bias
UNIT 3 **Science and Technology** Page 110	**CHAPTER 7** Stopping the Spread of Superbugs Page 112	Previewing a reading Scanning for information Recalling information Summarizing information **Reading Skill Focus:** Understanding graphics	Understanding meaning from context **Word Forms:** Recognizing the suffixes -tion and -ion Using common expressions and idioms	Discussing antibiotics Giving examples and sharing ideas Determining the author's purpose
	CHAPTER 8 It's Time for a Conversation: Learning the Language of Dolphins Page 130	Previewing a reading Scanning for information Recalling information Summarizing information **Reading Skill Focus:** Creating an outline	Understanding meaning from context **Word Forms:** Recognizing the suffix -ly Understanding synonyms	Discussing advantages and disadvantages Giving reasons for why you agree or disagree Assessing the author's tone

SCOPE & SEQUENCE

Unit & Theme	Chapter & Title	Reading Skills	Vocabulary Skills	Critical Thinking Skills
	CHAPTER 9 Space Science on Earth Page 148	Previewing a reading Scanning for information Recalling information Summarizing information **Reading Skill Focus:** Using headings to create an outline	Understanding meaning from context **Word Forms:** Recognizing the suffix -ful Understanding synonyms	Discussing and giving examples Discussing the benefits of technology Giving reasons for opinions Establishing the author's purpose
UNIT 4 **Government and History** Page 166	**CHAPTER 10** Antarctica: Whose Continent Is It Anyway? Page 168	Previewing a reading Scanning for information Recalling information Summarizing information **Reading Skill Focus:** Using headings to create an outline	Understanding meaning from context **Word Forms:** Recognizing the suffixes -ion and -tion Understanding synonyms	Discussing possible outcomes of the melting of Antarctica's ice caps Listing reasons why Antarctica is important Writing a set of guidelines for the protection of Antarctica Assessing the author's bias
	CHAPTER 11 The Mystery of the Iceman Page 186	Previewing a reading Scanning for information Recalling information Summarizing information **Reading Skill Focus:** Creating an information chart	Understanding meaning from context **Word Forms:** Identifying parts of speech: nouns and verbs Understanding useful phrases	Giving opinions Researching one of the ages of mankind and writing a description Assessing the author's tone and opinion
	CHAPTER 12 The Federal System of Government Page 204	Previewing a reading Scanning for information Recalling information Summarizing information **Reading Skill Focus:** Using headings to create an outline	Understanding meaning from context **Word Forms:** Recognizing the suffix -ment Understanding collocations	Drawing inferences from text Discussing the individuality of the 50 states Determining the author's purpose

PREFACE

Concepts for Today, Fourth Edition, is a reading skills text intended for high-intermediate, college-bound students of English-as-a-second- or foreign-language. The passages in this book are original articles drawn from a range of publications, thus allowing students the opportunity to read authentic materials from a wide variety of sources. As they engage with the materials in each chapter of this book, students develop the kinds of extensive and intensive reading skills they will need to achieve academic success in English.

Concepts for Today, Fourth Edition, is one in a series of five reading skills texts. The complete series has been designed to meet the needs of students from the beginning to the advanced levels and includes the following:

- *Reading for Today 1: Themes for Today*   beginning
- *Reading for Today 2: Insights for Today*   high-beginning
- *Reading for Today 3: Issues for Today*   intermediate
- *Reading for Today 4: Concepts for Today*   high-intermediate
- *Reading for Today 5: Topics for Today*   advanced

Concepts for Today, Fourth Edition, consists of four thematic units. Each unit contains three chapters that deal with related subjects. However, for maximum flexibility in the classroom, each chapter is independent, entirely separate in content from the other two chapters contained in that unit. Organizing the chapters into thematic units provides for a natural recycling of content-specific vocabulary and concepts, and discipline-specific sentence structure and rhetorical patterns. It should be noted that although all three chapters in each unit are linked by theme, they can as easily be taught individually as in concert with one another.

All of the chapters provide students with essential practice in the types of reading skills they will need in an academic environment. This practice requires students not only to read text, but also to examine information from various forms of charts, illustrations, and photographs. Furthermore, students are given the opportunity to speak and write about their own experiences, countries, and cultures in English and to compare these experiences and ideas with those of people from the United States and other countries.

The initial exercise preceding each reading encourages the students to think about the ideas, facts, and vocabulary that will be presented in the passage. Discussing unit and chapter illustrations in class helps students visualize what they are going to read about and gives them cues for the new vocabulary they will encounter. The exercises that follow the reading passage are intended to develop and improve reading proficiency, including the ability to learn new vocabulary from context and to develop comprehension of English sentence structure, and study skills such as note-taking and proper dictionary use. The follow-up activities give students the opportunity to master useful vocabulary encountered in the articles through discussion and group work and lead the students to a comprehension of main ideas and specific information.

New to the Fourth Edition

Concepts for Today, Fourth Edition, maintains the effective approach of the third edition with several significant improvements. This enhanced edition takes a more in-depth approach to vocabulary development and application by consistently introducing, practicing, and assessing vocabulary in context, while teaching valuable vocabulary-building skills that are recycled throughout the series.

The fourth edition of **Concepts for Today** contains six completely new chapters: *Learning through Video Games: Fact or Fiction, Sugar: A Not-So-Sweet Story, Traditional Medicine: A Non-Western Approach to Healing, Stopping the Spread of Superbugs, It's Time for a Conversation: Learning the Language of Dolphins,* and *Space Science on Earth*. In addition, the original remaining chapters have been updated to include current information.

There are several changes as well in the approach to learning vocabulary and acquiring specific reading skills in the new edition, and new exercises have been added. The first exercise is the original *Word Forms* exercise, which has been revised to include the context of the readings. A second new exercise, *Vocabulary Skills*, emphasizes various vocabulary skills, for example, dictionary skills, antonyms, synonyms, phrasal verbs, content-specific vocabulary, useful phrases, and collocations. A third new exercise, *Vocabulary in Context*, gives students additional practice in language from the chapter in a new context. A new *Reading Skill* section focuses on a specific reading skill, for example, understanding graphs, illustrations, and graphics, and creating charts, flowcharts, timelines, and Venn diagrams. Also new to the fourth edition is a *Critical Thinking* section, which includes questions about an author's purpose, tone, and bias. The activities in this section encourage students to use the information and vocabulary from the reading passages both orally and in writing, and to think beyond the reading passage and form their own opinions. In addition, the fourth edition includes new photos, graphs, and charts, all of which are designed to enhance students' comprehension of the readings. Finally, there is a crossword puzzle at the end of each chapter to reinforce vocabulary in that particular reading.

These revisions and enhancements to *Concepts for Today, Fourth Edition*, have been designed to help students improve their reading skills and develop confidence as they work through the text. At the same time, the fourth edition is structured so that teachers can observe students steadily progressing toward skillful, independent reading.

INTRODUCTION

How to Use This Book

Every chapter in this book consists of the following:

- *Prereading*
- *Reading*
- *Fact Finding*
- *Reading Analysis*
- *Vocabulary Skills*
- *Vocabulary in Context*
- *Reading Skill*
- *Information Recall*
- *Topics for Discussion and Writing*
- *Critical Thinking*
- *Crossword Puzzle*

The format of the chapters in the book is consistent. Although each chapter can be done entirely in class, some exercises may be assigned for homework. This, of course, depends on the individual teacher's preference, as well as the availability of class time. Each chapter consists of the following sections:

Prereading

The *Prereading* activity is designed to stimulate student interest and provide preliminary vocabulary for the passage itself. The importance of prereading should not be underestimated. Studies have shown the positive effect of prereading in motivating student interest, activating background knowledge, and enhancing reading comprehension. Time should be spent describing and discussing both unit and chapter photographs and illustrations as well as discussing the title and the prereading questions. Furthermore, students should try to relate the topic to their own experiences and try to predict what they are going to read about.

Reading

As students read the passage for the first time, they should be encouraged to read *ideas.* In English, ideas are in groups of words in sentences and in paragraphs, not in individual words.

Fact Finding

After the first reading, students will read the true/false statements, then go back to the passage and scan for the information that will clarify whether each statement is true or false. If the statement is false, students will rewrite the statement so that it becomes true. This activity can be done individually or in groups or pairs.

Reading Analysis

Students will read each question and answer it. This exercise deals with vocabulary from context, transition words, punctuation clues, sentence structure, sentence comprehension, and pronoun referents. The teacher should review personal and relative pronouns before doing this section. This exercise may be assigned for homework, or it may be done in class individually or in groups, giving the students the opportunity to discuss their reasons for their answers.

Vocabulary Skills

This section consists of two parts. The first part focuses on recognizing word forms. As an introduction to this exercise, it is recommended that teachers first review parts of speech, especially verbs, nouns, adjectives, and adverbs. Teachers should point out the position of each word form in a sentence. Students will develop a sense for which part of speech is missing in a given sentence. Teachers should also point out clues to verb form and number, and whether an idea is affirmative or negative. Each section has its own instructions, depending on the particular pattern that is being introduced. For example, in the section containing words that take -*tion* in the noun form, teachers can explain that in the exercise students will look at the verb and noun forms of these words. Teachers can use the examples in the directions for each chapter's *Recognizing Word Forms* section to see that the students understand the exercise. All of the sentences in this exercise are content specific, which not only helps reinforce the vocabulary, but also helps check the students' comprehension of the passage. This activity is very effective when done in pairs because students can discuss their answers. After students have a working knowledge of this type of exercise, it can be assigned for homework. The focus of Part 2 of the *Vocabulary Skills* section varies. The purpose of this section is to provide students with a range of ways to learn and practice new vocabulary, and make logical connections by working with words that are commonly paired or that are related to a particular topic. The exercises in this section focus on a variety of important vocabulary-related topics, such as antonyms, synonyms, phrasal verbs, content-specific vocabulary, collocations, and dictionary usage.

Vocabulary in Context

This is a fill-in exercise designed as a review of the vocabulary items covered in the *Reading Analysis* and/or the previous *Vocabulary Skills* exercises. In this exercise, the target words are used in new contexts, giving the students the opportunity for additional practice. It can be assigned for homework as a review or done in class as group work.

Reading Skill

Each chapter includes a new *Reading Skill* section, which provides instruction and practice with a specific reading skill, such as understanding line or bar graphs, or creating a flowchart, an outline, or a Venn diagram. This section is very effective when done in pairs or small groups. The exercises in these sections may also be done individually, but group work gives the students an opportunity to discuss their work.

Information Recall

This section requires students to review the passage again, in some cases along with the previous *Reading Skill* exercise, and answer questions that test the students' overall comprehension of the chapter. In addition, students must also write a short summary of the passage using no more than five sentences. In early chapters, the first sentence is given as a guide.

Topics for Discussion and Writing

This section provides ideas or questions for students to think about and work on alone, in pairs, or in small groups. Students are encouraged to use the information and vocabulary from the passages both orally and in their writing. The writing assignments may be done entirely in class, started in class and finished at home, or done entirely for homework. The last activity in this section is a journal-writing assignment that provides students with an opportunity to reflect on the topic of the chapter and respond to it in some personal way. Students should be encouraged to keep a journal and to write in it regularly. The students' journal writing may be purely personal, or students may choose to have the teacher read their entries. If the teacher reads the entries, the journals should be considered a free-writing activity and should be responded to rather than corrected.

Critical Thinking

This section contains various activities appropriate to the information in the passages. Some activities are designed for pair and small group work. Students are encouraged to use the information and vocabulary from the passages both orally and in writing. The critical thinking questions and activities provide students with an opportunity to think about some aspect of the chapter topic and to share their own thoughts and opinions about it. Additionally, students are asked to consider and discuss the author's purpose, tone, and/or bias. The goal of this section is for students to go beyond the reading itself and to form their own ideas and opinions on aspects of the topic. Teachers may also use these questions and activities as homework or in-class assignments. The activities in the *Critical Thinking* sections help students interact with the real world, as many exercises require students to go outside the classroom to collect specific information.

Crossword Puzzle

The *Crossword Puzzle* in each chapter is based on the vocabulary addressed in that chapter. Students can go over the puzzle orally if pronunciation practice with letters is needed. Teachers can have the students spell out their answers in addition to pronouncing the words themselves. Students invariably enjoy doing crossword puzzles. They are a fun way to reinforce the vocabulary presented in the various exercises in each chapter. Crossword puzzles also require students to pay attention to correct spelling. If the teacher prefers, students can do the *Crossword Puzzle* on their own or with a partner in their free time, or after they have completed an in-class assignment and are waiting for the rest of their classmates to finish.

Index of Key Words and Phrases

The *Index of Key Words and Phrases* is at the back of the book. This section contains words and phrases from all the chapters for easy reference. This index can help students locate words they need or wish to review. The words that are part of the Academic Word List are indicated with an icon.

Skills Index

The *Skills Index* lists the different skills presented and/or practiced in the book.

ACKNOWLEDGMENTS

The authors and publisher would like to thank the following reviewers:

Sola Armanious, Hudson County Community College; **Marina Broeder**, Mission College; **Kara Chambers**, Mission College; **Peter Chin**, Waseda University International; **Feri Collins**, BIR Training Center; **Courtney DeRouen**, University of Washington; **Jeanne de Simon**, University of West Florida; **Shoshana Dworkin**, BIR Training Center; **Cindy Etter**, University of Washington International and English Language Programs; **Ken Fackler**, University of Tennessee at Martin; **Jan Hinson**, Carson Newman University; **Chigusa Katoku**, Mission College; **Sharon Kruzic**, Mission College; **Carmella Lieskle**, Shimane University; **Yelena Malchenko**, BIR Training Center; **Mercedes Mont**, Miami Dade College; **Ewa Paluch**, BIR Training Center; **Barbara Pijan**, Portland State University, Intensive English Language Program; **Julaine Rosner**, Mission College; **Julie Scales**, University of Washington; **Mike Sfiropoulos**, Palm Beach State College; **Barbara Smith-Palinkas**, Hillsborough Community College; **Eileen Sotak**, BIR Training Center; **Matthew Watterson**, Hongik University; **Tristinn Williams**, IELP—University of Washington; **Iryna Zhylina**, Hudson County Community College; **Ana Zuljevic**, BIR Training Center

Acknowledgments from Authors
We are thankful to everyone at Cengage, especially Laura LeDréan, Mary Whittemore, Jennifer Monaghan, Patricia Giunta, and Lori Solbakken for their unwavering support. We are extremely grateful to all the teachers and students who use our book and who never hesitate to give us such incredible feedback. As always, we are very appreciative of the ongoing encouragement from our families, friends, and colleagues.

L.C.S and N.N.M.

Dedication:

To our parents: Peg and Smitty; Anthony and Antoinette

Living in Society

Students using technology in
the modern classroom

1. How do children learn? What types of technology might help them learn better?

2. How are families different today than they were in the past?

3. Are you a happy person? What makes you happy? Do you think happiness is genetic?

CHAPTER 1

Learning through Video Games:
Fact or Fiction?

Prereading

1. Did you ever use video games in school? Do you think they are useful in the classroom? Why or why not?

2. Do you think children can learn from computer games, or do you think they do not help learning? If so, why do you think so? If not, why not?

3. Read the title of this article, and look at the photo. Where are these children? What do you think they are doing? Why?

Reading

🎧 **Read the passage carefully. Then complete the exercises that follow.**

Learning through Video Games: Fact or Fiction?

Video games are a major part of children's lives today, and they spend hours playing them. However, parents and teachers alike question the educational value of video games at home and in the classroom. Even more importantly, can playing video games, specifically violent ones, actually be harmful to children? This chapter
5 presents two articles with different perspectives on the topic.

The First Perspective: Gaming to Learn
Do educational computer and video games lead to real learning gains?
by Amy Novotney, *American Psychological Association*

Many of today's K–12 students are spending their class time—and a lot of it—exploring science and writing sentences through the website BrainPOP. The website allows kids to watch movies, complete quizzes, and play games covering hundreds of topics within math, science, social studies, English, technology, art,
10 music, and health.
BrainPOP is just one of hundreds of educational game websites in a billion-dollar industry that is growing in popularity. Nearly 60 percent of teachers now use digital games at least weekly in teaching, with 18 percent using them daily, according to a nationwide survey of 488 K–12 teachers conducted by researchers
15 at New York University and the University of Michigan. But despite the growing popularity of such games, research has yet to determine whether they really help children learn.
Over the past 20 years, scientists have conducted nine major reviews of research on the effectiveness of educational computer and video games. Overall, they've
20 found that the research on games is highly diverse, disorganized, and unfocused. Douglas Clark, Ph.D., professor of the learning sciences education at Vanderbilt University says, "The research shows that games as a medium can be effective, but not always. Design is really what matters. Nobody assumes that all lectures, labs, or books are good simply because of their medium." Jan Plass, Ph.D., a professor in
25 NYU's Steinhardt School of Culture, Education and Human Development and one of the study's lead authors, agrees. "We found that well-designed games can motivate students to learn less popular subjects, such as math, and that game-based learning can actually get students interested in the subject matter."

Psychologists are also studying a learning game for college students. A series
of studies were conducted by psychologist Art Graesser, Ph.D., of the Institute
for Intelligent Systems at the University of Memphis, and his colleagues, who
developed the game. They reported improvements in critical thinking skills among
students at three different types of higher education institutions—a community
college, a state university, and a private college. "Every part of the game was backed
by one or more principles of learning," says Graesser. "That's different from a lot of
commercial games that often try to improve motivation but not learning. We really
tried to do both."

The Second Perspective: Review finds video game play may provide learning, health, and social benefits

by Lisa Bowen, *American Psychological Association*

Playing video games, including violent games, may boost children's learning,
health, and social skills, according to a review of research in *American Psychologist*.
The study comes out as debate continues among psychologists and other health
professionals regarding the effects of violent media on youth.

While one view maintains that playing video games is intellectually lazy, such play
actually may strengthen a range of cognitive skills such as spatial navigation, reasoning,
memory, and perception, according to several studies reviewed in the article.

Playing video games may also help children develop problem-solving skills. The
more adolescents reported playing strategic video games, the more they improved in
problem solving and school grades the following year. Children's creativity was also
enhanced by playing any kind of video game, including violent games, but not when
the children used other forms of technology, such as a computer or cell phone, other
research revealed.

Simple games that are easy to access and can be played quickly can improve
players' moods, promote relaxation, and ward off anxiety, the study said. "If playing
video games simply makes people happier, this seems to be a fundamental emotional
benefit to consider," said Isabela Granic, Ph.D., of Radboud University Nijmegen in
the Netherlands.

The authors also highlighted the possibility that video games are effective tools
for learning resilience, or flexibility, in the face of failure. By learning to cope with
ongoing failures in games, the authors suggest that children build emotional resilience
they can rely upon in their everyday lives.

Another stereotype the research challenges is the socially isolated gamer. More
than 70 percent of gamers play with a friend. Multiplayer games become virtual
social communities, where decisions need to be made quickly about whom to trust or
reject and how to lead a group, the authors said. People who play video games that
encourage cooperation, even if the games are violent, are more likely to be helpful

65 to others while gaming than those who play the same games competitively, a recent study found.

Perhaps a compromise between the two perspectives is to have adults monitor or screen video games before allowing younger children to play them. Another helpful strategy is to limit how much time children are allowed to play the games each day.

70 Finally, adults, especially parents, can discuss the video games with their children and explain why some games are better to play than others.

Fact Finding

Read the passage again. Then read the following statements. Check (√) whether each statement is True or False. If a statement is false, rewrite it so that it is true. Then go back to the passage and find the line that supports your answer.

1. _√_ True _____ False   ~~Most~~ *Some* research shows that playing video games helps children learn.

   _____

2. _√_ True _____ False   A majority of K–12 teachers use video games in the classroom.

   _____

3. _____ True _____ False   All video games motivate students to learn less popular subjects.

   _____

4. _√_ True _____ False   Some video games can improve critical thinking skills in college students.

   _____

5. _____ True _√_ False   Playing violent video games decreases children's ability to learn.

   _____

6. _____ True _√_ False   Most video gamers play video games alone.

   _____

7. _√_ True _____ False   Parents and teachers should pay attention to which games the children are playing.

   _____

Reading Analysis

Read each question carefully. Circle the letter or the number of the correct answer, or write your answer in the space provided.

1. Read lines 2–4.
   a. **Alike** means
      1. the same.
      2. both.
      3. always.
   b. **Specifically** means
      1. sometimes.
      2. mostly.
      3. especially.

2. In the question that introduces the first perspective, **learning gains** means
   a. improvements in learning.
   b. better teachers.
   c. more time playing video games.

3. Read lines 6–7. **K–12** students are
   a. in elementary school.
   b. in high school.
   c. in kindergarten.
   d. all of the above.

4. Read lines 11–12. **A billion-dollar industry** is
   a. a business that spends a lot of money.
   b. a business that makes a lot of money.
   c. a new kind of business.

5. Read lines 15–17.
   a. **Despite** means
      1. because of.
      2. although.
      3. as a result of.
   b. **But despite the growing popularity of such games, research has yet to determine whether they really help children learn.**
      This sentence means
      1. research has determined that video games really help children learn.
      2. research has not determined if video games really help children learn.
      3. research has determined that video games don't really help children learn.

6. Read lines 19–20. This sentence means that the research on games is
   a. easy to understand.
   b. important.
   c. confusing.

7. In line 22, **medium** means
   a. method.
   b. size.
   c. idea.

8. In line 26, **motivate** means
   a. help.
   b. encourage.
   c. ask.

9. In line 38, **boost** means
   a. increase.
   b. hurt.
   c. change.

10. Read lines 40–41.
   a. **Debate** means
      1. interest.
      2. research.
      3. disagreement.
   b. What is this debate about?
      1. The benefits of playing computer games in the classroom
      2. The effects of spending too much time playing video games
      3. The results of violent video games on young people

11. Read lines 42–44.
   a. In this sentence, **view** means
      1. opinion.
      2. scene.
      3. reason.
   b. **Cognitive skills** are used for
      1. moving.
      2. thinking.
      3. feeling.

12. In line 48, **enhanced** means
   a. learned.
   b. discussed.
   c. improved.

13. Read lines 51–55.

    a. **Ward off** means

        1. protect against.

        2. help with.

        3. turn off.

    b. **Fundamental** means

        1. useful.

        2. necessary.

        3. intelligent.

    c. Playing simple video games can have a fundamental emotional benefit if

        1. the games are violent.

        2. the games make the player feel happy.

        3. the games can be played quickly.

14. Read lines 56–59.

    a. In these sentences, a synonym for **resilience** is

    flexibility .

    b. **Cope** means

        1. manage.

        2. understand.

        3. learn.

15. Read lines 60–61.

    a. A **socially isolated gamer** is someone who

        1. plays a lot of video games.

        2. plays video games alone.

        3. plays video games with friends.

    b. Do most gamers play alone or with a friend?

        1. Alone

        2. With a friend

16. Read lines 67–69.

    a. Two people or two groups **compromise** when they

        1. negotiate and reach an agreement.

        2. cannot agree on an idea.

        3. have an argument.

    b. **Monitor** means

        1. check on something.

        2. understand something.

        3. stop something.

c. What is the compromise in this sentence?
    1. Adults should not allow children to play violent video games.
    2. Children should be allowed to play violent video games.
    3. Adults should watch the video games before the children play them.
d. A **strategy** is a
    1. perspective.
    2. plan.
    3. limit.

17. What is the main idea of the passage?
    a. Parents and teachers do not want children to play video games, especially violent ones.
    b. Many teachers use video games in their classroom, and research seems to support their effectiveness in improving student learning.
    c. Although research has not conclusively shown that video games improve learning, teachers use them anyway.

Vocabulary Skills

PART 1

Recognizing Word Forms

In English, some nouns become adjectives by adding the suffix -al, for example, *tradition (n.)*, *traditional (adj.)*.

Complete each sentence with the correct word form on the left. The nouns may be singular or plural.

education *(n.)*   1. Researchers question whether video games are a useful

educational *(adj.)*   _____ tool. In other words, can video games be helpful to

      _____?

emotion *(n.)*   2. Players often have different _____ when they play video

emotional *(adj.)*   games. Some people are happy and relaxed when they play, which is an

      _____ benefit of gaming.

motivation *(n.)*

motivational *(adj.)*

3. Some teachers believe that using computer games in the classroom improves _n_____es_____ for students to learn less popular subjects. However, not all games are _adj_____ .

profession *(n.)*

professional *(adj.)*

4. People in _h_____es_____ such as education and health study the use of violent video games by children. Many _adj_____ educators debate the effects of violent media on young people.

psychology *(n.)*

psychological *(adj.)*

5. Other researchers in the field of _n_____ are studying the effectiveness of a learning game for college students. They are examining the _adj_____ effects that the games may have on the students' critical thinking skills.

PART 2

Antonyms

Antonyms are words with different or opposite meanings. For example, *allow* and *prohibit* are antonyms.

Read each sentence. Write the antonym of the word in parentheses in the space provided.

8 alike	enhanced	7 monitor	resilience
5 boosts	gain	motivate 6	specifically
10 despite	isolated 1		

1. Parents sometimes fear that children who play video games are _____ because they appear to be playing alone. *(grouped)*

2. Teachers question whether the use of computer games in the classroom will lead to a(n) _____ in learning. *(loss)*

3. Some believe that playing video games can help children to learn _____ when they fail. *(inflexibility)*

4. Parents and teachers _____ question the educational value of video games. *(different)*

5. According to the American Psychological Association, playing video games

_____ a child's health and social skills. (*decreases*)

6. Well-designed computer games may _____ students to learn less popular subjects. (*discourage*)

7. Parents are advised to _____ the types of computer games that their children play. (*ignore*)

8. Some researchers found that creativity was also _____ by playing any kind of video game, including violent games. (*worsened*)

9. _____ the growing popularity of video games, research still hasn't determined if they are helpful to learning. (*because of*)

10. Many parents worry that playing video games, _____ violent ones, can actually be harmful for children. (*generally*)

Vocabulary in Context

Read the following sentences. Complete each sentence with the correct word or phrase from the box. Use each word or phrase only once.

cope *(v.)*	enhanced *(v.)*	resilience *(n.)*	views *(n.)*
debate *(n.)*	fundamental *(adj.)*	specifically *(adv.)*	ward off *(v.)*
despite *(prep.)*	motivated *(v.)*		

1. Carolyn's experience as a sickly child _____ her to become a doctor.

2. _____ the cold weather, I am going to take a walk on the beach.

3. My parents have different _____ about the best place to live. My mother prefers to live in the city, but my father prefers the countryside.

4. I always put insect repellent on my arms and legs to _____ mosquitoes when I go to the park.

5. Being a good reader is _____ to being a good learner.

6. The small tree bent but did not break during the storm. Because of its

_____ , it continued to thrive.

7. The music _____ the play and made the experience even more enjoyable.

8. Many pets, _____ cats and dogs, are often treated like family by their owners.

9. It was very difficult for people in the town to _____ after the terrible earthquake. Many of them had lost their homes.

10. Instructors often _____ the use of cell phones in the classroom. Some think they can be useful, but others find them distracting.

Reading Skill

Understanding Charts

Charts contain important information. Charts often compare numbers or amounts and help you understand important information from a reading passage.

Read the bar graph and pie chart below. Then answer the questions.

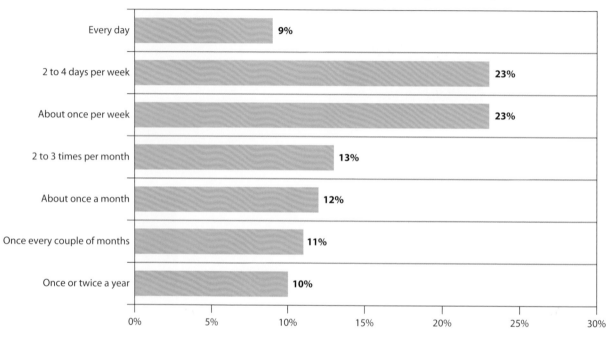

How frequently do students use computer games in your classroom?

Every day	9%
2 to 4 days per week	23%
About once per week	23%
2 to 3 times per month	13%
About once a month	12%
Once every couple of months	11%
Once or twice a year	10%

Source: gamesandlearning.org
Among K–8 teachers who use digital games in teaching (N=513)

1. How many K–8 teachers participated in the survey?
   a. 56
   b. 100
   c. 513

2. What percent of teachers use computer games in their classrooms once a week or more?
   a. 9%
   b. 46%
   c. 55%

3. What percent of teachers use computer games in their classrooms once a month or less?

    a. 12%

    b. 25%

    c. 33%

4. What percent of teachers almost never use computer games in their classrooms?

    a. 10%

    b. 11%

    c. 12%

How do you typically have your students use digital games?

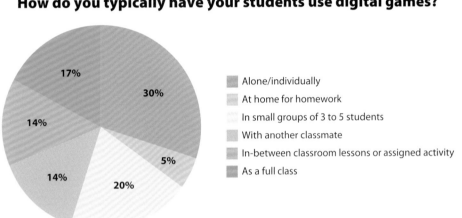

Source: gamesandlearning.org
Among K – 8 teachers who use digital games in teaching (N=513)

1. What percent of students use digital games at home for homework?

    a. 5%

    b. 14%

    c. 30%

2. What percent of students use digital games with one or more partners?

    a. 14%

    b. 20%

    c. 34%

3. What percent of students use digital games by themselves?

    a. 14%

    b. 30%

    c. 44%

Information Recall

Read the passage again, and review the charts. Then answer the questions.

1. What were the scientists' conclusions about the effectiveness of computer games as a learning tool?

   _____

   _____

   _____

2. How often do most teachers use digital games in teaching?

   _____

   _____

   _____

3. What are some of the benefits of playing video games?

   _____

   _____

   _____

4. What is a possible compromise between people who disagree about allowing children to play video games in and out of the classroom?

   _____

   _____

   _____

Writing a Summary

A summary is a short paragraph that provides the most important information from a reading. It usually does not include details, just the main ideas. When you write a summary, it is important to use your own words and not copy directly from the reading.

Write a brief summary of the passage. It should not be more than five sentences. Use your own words. The first two sentences of the summary are below. Write three more sentences to complete the summary.

Children enjoy playing video games. However, parents and teachers wonder if they

help children learn.

Topics for Discussion and Writing

1. Did any of your teachers use video games in the classroom? If so, did they help you learn? How? If not, do you wish they had used video games? Why or why not?

2. Some parents worry that children spend too much time playing video games. Do you think this is true? How much time each week do you think children should be allowed to play video games? Discuss this with a partner, then compare your answers with your classmates' answers.

3. Write in your journal. What do you think are some reasons why video games, specifically violent ones, are so popular with children and adults? Give reasons for your opinion.

Critical Thinking

1. Imagine that you can design a video game to enhance student learning. Describe the game and explain why you think it will be a useful learning tool.

2. According to a review of research in *American Psychologist*, playing video games, including violent games, may boost children's learning, health, and social skills. Do you think this gain justifies allowing children to play violent games? Explain the reasons for your answer.

3. How do you think Lisa Bowen, the author of "Review finds video game play may provide learning, health, and social benefits," (p. 5–7) feels about younger children playing video games? What makes you think this?

Crossword Puzzle

Review the words in the box below. Then read the clues on the next page. Write the words in the correct spaces in the puzzle.

alike	debate	industry	motivates
boost	despite	isolated	specifically
cognitive	enhanced	medium	strategy
compromise	fundamental	monitor	view
cope	gains		

Crossword Puzzle Clues

ACROSS CLUES

2. The use of video games in the classroom is only one _____ for teaching children.

4. Children gain social skills by learning to _____ with failure when playing video games.

6. Parents need to screen the video games their children play, _____ the violent games.

9. Being able to play video games often _____ children to learn because they are having fun while learning.

11. Playing video games has a _____ benefit: it makes people feel relaxed.

14. A(n) _____ is a business.

15. Adults and children _____ enjoy playing video games. They both use their computers for fun.

16. Children's _____, or thinking, skills are improved through active learning.

17. Most children are not _____ when they play video games. Most often, they play with at least one friend.

18. Parents and teachers need to have a clear _____ for the use of video games at home and in the classroom.

DOWN CLUES

1. Some research seems to show that playing video games can _____, or improve, children's thinking skills.

3. The _____ for and against allowing children to play violent video games is not likely to end soon.

5. Parents and teachers usually have the same _____, or perspective, on how children learn best.

7. Parents may wish to _____ on having their children play video games by selecting the ones they permit their children to have.

8. _____ the ongoing research on video games, scientists have not proven that they are truly effective in helping children learn.

10. Some research shows that children's creativity is _____ by playing video games.

12. When parents _____ what their children play, they make choices about which games to allow them to have.

13. Researchers need to conduct studies that will show positive learning _____ among children who play video games.

Prereading

1. Read the title of the passage. What is "birth order"?

2. Some people believe that birth order affects an individual's personality or intelligence. What do you think about this idea?

3. Work as a class and in groups to complete the following activities.

   a. How many brothers and sisters do you have? Are you the youngest? Are you the oldest? Are you an only child? Make a chart on the board of how many students in the class are only children, firstborn, second born, third born, youngest, etc.

   b. Form groups according to birth order; in other words, all the *only children* will form one group, all the *firstborns* will form another group, etc. In your groups, describe your personalities. Make a list of the personality characteristics that are common to all of you.

   c. Put your responses on the board. Discuss your answers as a class. What similarities are there in personalities for students with the same birth order?

Reading

🎧 **Read the passage carefully. Then complete the exercises that follow.**

The Birth-Order Myth

by Alfie Kohn, *Health*

"No wonder he's so charming and funny—he's the baby of the family!" "She works hard trying to please the boss. I bet she's a firstborn." "Anyone that selfish has to be an only child."

It's long been part of *folk wisdom* that birth order strongly affects personality,
5   intelligence, and achievement. However, most of the research claiming that firstborns are radically different from other children has been discredited, and it now seems that any effects of birth order on intelligence or personality will likely be washed out by all the other influences in a person's life. In fact, the belief in the permanent impact of birth order, according to Toni Falbo, a social psychologist at the University of Texas
10   at Austin, "comes from the psychological theory that your personality is fixed by the time you're six. That assumption simply is incorrect."

The better, later, and larger studies are less likely to find birth order a useful predictor of anything. When two Swiss social scientists, Cecile Ernst and Jules Angst, reviewed 1,500 studies a few years ago, they concluded that "birth-order differences
15   in personality . . . are nonexistent in our sample. In particular, there is no evidence for a 'firstborn personality.'"

Putting Birth Order in Context

Of the early studies that seemed to show birth order mattered, most failed to recognize how other factors could confuse the issue. Take family size: Plenty of surveys showed that eldest children were overrepresented among high achievers. However, that
20   really says less about being a firstborn than about not having many siblings, or any at all. After all, any group of firstborns is going to include a disproportionate number of children from small families since every family has a firstborn, but fewer have a fourth born. Most experts now believe that position in the family means little when taken out of the context of *everything* going on in a particular household—whether sibling rivalry
25   is promoted or discouraged, for instance. Parents who believe that firstborns are more capable or deserving may treat them differently, thus setting up a self-fulfilling prophecy.

Old Theories Die Hard

Consider the question of whether birth order affects achievement or intelligence. Many experts today suggest that birth order plays no role at all. When Judith Blake, a demographer at the University of California, Los Angeles, looked at birth patterns

30   before 1938 and compared them to SAT[1] scores for that group of children, she found
no connection. On the other hand, the *number* of siblings does matter. "Small families
are, on average, much more supportive of the kind of verbal ability that helps people
succeed in school," Blake says. The reason, she believes, is that parental attention is
diluted in larger families.

35   As for effects on personality, results are mixed. Research suggests that you're
somewhat more likely to be outgoing, well adjusted, and independent if you grew
up with few or no siblings. Two recent studies, however, found no differences on the
basis of size alone. The only certainty is that there don't seem to be any *disadvantages*
to growing up in a small family—including being an only child. After reviewing
40   141 studies, Falbo and a colleague found that being raised with or without siblings
doesn't affect personality in predictable ways. Where small differences were found—
such as in achievement motivation—they favored the only children.

Do Kids Need More Space?

If position doesn't control destiny and family size has only a minor impact, what
about spacing between children? Although little research has been conducted, some
45   psychologists believe there are more advantages to having kids far apart rather than close
together. Some specialists caution that siblings close in age may be treated as a single unit.

This is eyebrow-raising news, given that parents are sometimes advised not to wait
too long before having a second child. However, different studies have led to different
conclusions. One found that a firstborn was more likely to have high self-esteem if his
50   or her sibling was *less* than two years younger. Another indicated that spacing had no
impact on social competence, and others note positive effects for boys but not for girls.

As with birth order, cautions about jumping to conclusions may be ignored by the
general public. As Blake says, "You're never going to completely put to rest what
people think is fun to believe."

---

[1] The **SAT** is the Scholastic Aptitude Test. The scores on this test are used to determine high school students' ability to do college work.

Fact Finding

Read the passage again. Then read the following statements. Check (√) whether each statement is True or False. If a statement is false, rewrite it so that it is true. Then go back to the passage and find the line that supports your answer.

1. _____ True _____ False   The firstborn child in the family is different from the other children in the family.

2. _____ True _____ False   Studies will probably find that birth order affects personality.

3. _____ True _____ False   The number of children in a family affects personality more than birth order does.

4. _____ True _____ False   Growing up in a small family has many disadvantages.

5. _____ True _____ False   Many experts believe that birth order does not affect intelligence.

6. _____ True _____ False   Some people believe it is better for a family to have children far apart rather than close in age.

Reading Analysis

Read each question carefully. Circle the letter or the number of the correct answer, or write your answer in the space provided.

1. Read lines 1–3.
   a. What follows the dash (—)?
      1. The reason he's charming and funny
      2. Extra information about him
      3. Information about his family
   b. **He's the baby of the family** means
      1. he's very young.
      2. he's the youngest child.
      3. he's very immature.
   c. A **selfish** person
      1. has younger brothers or sisters.
      2. takes care of his or her siblings.
      3. only thinks about himself or herself.

2. Read the first paragraph. These statements are examples of
   a. the author's beliefs.
   b. birth-order myths.
   c. facts about birth order.

3. Read lines 5–8.
   a. **Discredited** means
      1. proved to be correct.
      2. misunderstood.
      3. found to be wrong.
   b. **Influences** means
      1. effects.
      2. beliefs.
      3. differences.
   c. This statement means that, as a result of other influences, the effects of birth order
      1. will disappear.
      2. will become clear.
      3. will combine.

4. Read lines 8–11.
   a. What information follows **in fact**?
      1. True information about birth order
      2. Information about Toni Falbo
      3. Information to support the previous idea

b. In line 8, **impact** means
   1. importance.
   2. effect.
   3. cause.
c. What word in these sentences is a synonym for **assumption**?
   1. Influence
   2. Belief
   3. Fact

5. Read lines 13–16.
   a. What do the dots between **personality** and **are** indicate?
      1. Some words have been deleted.
      2. Both Ernst and Angst are speaking at the same time.
      3. It is a quotation.
   b. **Nonexistent** means that something
      1. is not important.
      2. is different.
      3. doesn't exist.
   c. **In particular** means
      1. part of.
      2. specifically.
      3. in addition.
   d. **Evidence** means
      1. ideas.
      2. proof.
      3. reason.

6. Read lines 18–19.
   a. **Take family size.** In this sentence, **take** means
      1. decide.
      2. criticize.
      3. consider.
   b. **Plenty of** means
      1. some.
      2. a lot of.
      3. a few.

7. Read lines 23–25.
   a. Why is ***everything*** in italics?
      1. To show importance
      2. Because it's a new word
      3. To indicate a large number

b. The author means that
   1. sibling rivalry is important.
   2. position in the family is important.
   3. all things that are going on are important.
c. What is the purpose of the dash (—) after **household**?
   1. To add extra information
   2. To give an example
   3. To give a definition
d. **Sibling rivalry** means
   1. competition between brothers and sisters.
   2. arguments between parents.
   3. spacing between brothers and sisters.
e. **Promoted** and **discouraged** are
   1. antonyms.
   2. synonyms.

8. Read lines 25–26.
   a. This sentence means that, if parents treat their firstborns differently from their siblings,
      1. the firstborns will grow up the way their parents expect.
      2. the firstborns will become very unhappy when they grow up.
      3. the firstborns will become very happy when they grow up.
   b. A **prophecy** is
      1. a prediction.
      2. an opinion.
      3. an influence.
   c. A **self-fulfilling prophecy** means that someone's expectations of you
      1. may affect your behavior and make the prophecy become true.
      2. may make you be able to predict your own future.
      3. may make you have certain beliefs.

9. Read lines 28–31.
   a. What is the **SAT**?

   _____

   b. Where did you find this information?

   _____

   c. This type of information is called
      1. an abbreviation.
      2. a footnote.
      3. an asterisk.

d. **On the other hand** indicates
   1. more information.
   2. an example.
   3. an opposing idea.

e. Why is *number* in italics?

---

10. Read lines 33–34. **Diluted** means

a. increased.

b. reduced.

c. changed.

11. Read lines 35–38.

a. **Results are mixed** means
   1. different people got different results.
   2. everyone got the same results.
   3. different people were confused about their results.

b. **Mixed** means
   1. confused.
   2. varied.
   3. combined.

12. Read lines 43–44. **Spacing between children** means

a. how far apart children stand.

b. how far apart children are in age.

c. how far apart children are from their parents.

13. Read lines 47–48. **Eyebrow-raising news** is

a. wonderful.

b. terrible.

c. surprising.

14. In lines 52–53, **jumping to conclusions** means

a. deciding something without having enough facts.

b. believing something is incorrect.

c. trying to find out reasons for something.

15. What is the main idea of the passage?

a. Birth order affects personality, achievement, and intelligence.

b. Birth order and spacing between children have no effect on a person's personality, achievement, or intelligence.

c. Some people like to believe that birth order affects personality although there is no evidence of this.

Vocabulary Skills

Recognizing Word Forms

In English, some adjectives become nouns by deleting a final -t and adding -ce, for example, *important (adj.), importance (n.)*.

Complete each sentence with the correct word form on the left. All the nouns are singular.

competent (adj.)

competence (n.)

1. One birth-order study concluded that spacing between siblings affected their _____ in social situations. Another study found that boys were more _____ than girls. Different studies have different conclusions.

intelligent (adj.)

intelligence (n.)

2. Some people believe that firstborns are more _____ than their siblings. Others believe that birth order does not have an effect on _____ .

evident (adj.)

evidence (n.)

3. According to Cecile Ernst and Jules Angst, there is no _____ for a firstborn personality. In other words, specific personality traits were not _____ in all firstborns.

significant (adj.)

significance (n.)

4. Judith Blake found no _____ differences in SAT scores between siblings depending on their birth order. She believes that the number of children in a family is of greater _____ in predicting differences in test scores.

different (adj.)

difference (n.)

5. Most research has found that firstborns are not _____ from other children. In other words, there is no _____ in personality and achievement according to birth order.

PART 2

Using a Dictionary

In English, words may have more than one meaning, depending on the context. For example, *space* may refer to the area beyond Earth (*The exploration of space has helped us learn about the solar system.*). It may also mean a blank or empty area (*There is a lot of space between the sofa and the TV.*). In addition, *space* can mean a place used for something (*We put extra boxes in a space in the closet.*).

1. Read the following sentence. Use the context to help you understand the word in bold. Then read the dictionary entry for **position**, and circle the appropriate definition.

   Most experts now believe that **position** in the family means little when taken out of the context of *everything* going on in a particular household—whether sibling rivalry is promoted or discouraged, for instance.

   > **position** /pə'zɪʃən/ *n.* **1** a location, a point where s.t. exists or belongs: *The best position for that desk is against the wall.* **2** the way in which s.o or s.t. is arranged: *He was sitting in an uncomfortable position.*‖*I moved the bolt on the door into the locked position.* **3** a job, employment: *She has an excellent position as the head of a school.* **4** a rank among others, place in an order: *That student holds the top position in his class.*

2. Circle the letter of the sentence that has the appropriate meaning of **position**.
   a. Most experts now believe that one's job in the family means little when taken out of the context of *everything* going on in a particular household.
   b. Most experts now believe that the point where one exists in the family means little when taken out of the context of *everything* going on in a particular household.
   c. Most experts now believe that one's order in the family means little when taken out of the context of *everything* going on in a particular household.
   d. Most experts now believe that the way one is arranged in the family means little when taken out of the context of *everything* going on in a particular household.

3. An **order** in the family refers to
   a. where someone belongs.
   b. how someone is employed.
   c. whether one is born first, second, etc.

4. Read the following sentence. Use the context to help you understand the word in bold. Then read the dictionary entry for **promote**, and circle the appropriate definition.

Some parents **promote** sibling rivalry among their children.

> **promote** /prə'moʊt/ v. [T] **-moted, -moting, -motes 1** to advance in rank, give s.o. a better job: *Her boss promoted her to supervisor in accounting.* **2** to make known to the public, advertise goods and services: *The marketing department promoted our new product in television commercials.* **3** to support, propose, esp. for the public good: *The mayor promoted the idea of building a new sports stadium in the city. -adj.* **promotable**.

5. Circle the letter of the sentence that has the appropriate meaning of **promote**.
   a. Some parents advertise sibling rivalry among their children.
   b. Some parents support sibling rivalry among their children.
   c. Some parents advance sibling rivalry in rank among their children.

6. **Promote** means
   a. advance.
   b. make public.
   c. encourage.

Vocabulary in Context

Read the following sentences. Complete each sentence with the correct word or phrase from the box. Use each word or phrase only once.

assumption *(n.)*	impact *(n.)*	nonexistent *(adj.)*	plenty of
discouraged *(adj.)*	in particular	on the other hand	selfish *(adj.)*
evidence *(n.)*	influenced *(v.)*		

1. Would you like to stay for dinner? There is _____ food here for all of us.

2. My parents _____ me from going to a university in another country. They wanted me to go to a college near my home.

3. Cara believes that she will get a good job if she learns English. Because of this

   _____ , she started taking English classes this semester.

4. Marco likes all kinds of sports, but he enjoys soccer _____.

5. Daniel is not a _____ person at all. He is very kind and generous, and he is always helpful to his friends.

6. Last year's hurricane had a big _____ on a lot of people in that city. There was no electricity or water in many homes, and the buses and trains did not run for several months.

7. People cannot survive in places on Earth where water is _____.

8. The police carefully study _____ at crime scenes, such as fingerprints or blood.

9. My parents are both teachers. Their love for education _____ me to become a teacher, too.

10. Carol is not sure what she is going to do on her vacation. She is thinking about taking

    a trip to visit some friends. _____, she may stay home and relax with her family.

Reading Skill

Using Headings to Create an Outline

Readings often have headings. Headings introduce new ideas or topics. They also introduce details. Using headings to make an outline can help you understand and remember the most important information from the reading.

Read the article again. Underline the headings. Then scan the article and complete the following outline, using the sentences that you have underlined to help you. You will use this outline later to answer specific questions about the article.

I. The Myth and the Reality about Birth Order

    A. The Myth: _____

    B. The Reality: _____

II. _____

    A. The findings of Cecile Ernst and Jules Angst
_____

        1. Birth-order differences in personality are nonexistent.
_____

        2. _____

    B. _____

        1. Birth order does not affect intelligence; she looked at birth patterns before 1938 and compared them to SAT scores for that group of children, and she found no connection.

III. _____

    A. _____

        1. It does affect intelligence; small families tend to be more supportive of the kind of verbal ability that helps people succeed in school.

    B. _____

        1. Parents who believe that firstborns are more capable or deserving may treat them differently, thus setting up a self-fulfilling prophecy.

    C. _____

        1. Some psychologists believe there are more advantages to having kids far apart.

        2. One study found that a firstborn was more likely to have high self-esteem if his or her sibling was less than two years younger.

IV. _____

    A. You're more likely to be outgoing, well adjusted, and independent if you grew up with few

       or no siblings.

    B. _____

    C. One study indicated that spacing had no impact on social competence.

Information Recall

Review the information in the outline above. Then answer the questions.

1. What do many people believe about birth order?

_____

_____

2. What is the truth about birth order?

_____

_____

3. What were the research results about birth order?

_____

_____

4. What are three family factors that may have more of an effect on personality and intelligence than birth order? Name and briefly describe each one.

    a. _____

    b. _____

    c. _____

5. Did all the research on family size and spacing have the same results? Explain your answer.

_____

_____

Writing a Summary

A summary is a short paragraph that provides the most important information in a reading. It usually does not include details, just the main ideas. When you write a summary, it is important to use your own words and not copy directly from the reading.

Write a brief summary of the passage. It should not be more than five sentences. Use your own words. The first two sentences of the summary are below. Write three more sentences to complete the summary.

Although people like to believe that our birth order affects our personality, research has proven that this myth is incorrect. In fact, birth order doesn't seem to predict anything about a person.

Topics for Discussion and Writing

1. What stereotypes do you have in your country about children and birth order? How do you think these ideas came about?

2. Refer to the Birth-Order Survey on the next page. As a class, add more pairs of adjectives to complete the survey. After you have finished, go outside your class alone or in pairs. Survey two or three people. Then bring back your data, and combine it with the other students' information.
   a. What was your opinion about birth-order myths *before* you did your surveys and read this article? Do you still have that opinion?
   b. Does the information you collected support the author's findings or conflict with them? Give reasons for your answer.

3. Write in your journal. What do you think are the advantages and disadvantages of being an only child? Explain your opinion. Indicate if you are an only child or whether or not you would like to be an only child.

Birth-Order Survey

The purpose of this questionnaire is to collect data regarding birth order. Please answer the following questions.

1. Do you have siblings? How many? _____

2. What is your order of birth? That is, are you an *only child, firstborn, second born, third born*? Are you also the youngest child?

   _____

3. Choose one word from each pair of adjectives below that best describes your personality. Then add more adjectives to describe your personality.

1. anxious / confident	13. mature / immature
2. patient / impatient	14. funny / serious
3. boring / interesting	15. _____
4. talkative / quiet	16. _____
5. understanding / insensitive	17. _____
6. diligent / lazy	18. _____
7. friendly / disagreeable	19. _____
8. competitive / cooperative	20. _____
9. considerate / thoughtless	21. _____
10. creative / unimaginative	22. _____
11. curious / indifferent	23. _____
12. dependent / independent	24. _____

Critical Thinking

1. The author writes, "Parents who believe that firstborns are more capable or deserving may treat them differently, thus setting up a self-fulfilling prophecy." How do you think parents influence their children by treating them differently?

2. According to Judith Blake, the number of siblings a person has affects his or her personality because parental attention is diluted in larger families. Do you agree with this theory? Explain your answer.

3. In the last paragraph of the article on page 24, Judith Blake states that conclusions about birth order may be ignored by the general public. Why does she believe that people might ignore these findings? What do you think her opinion is about the general public?

Crossword Puzzle

Review the words in the box below. Then read the clues on the next page. Write the words in the correct spaces in the puzzle.

assumption	firstborn	predict	SAT
diluted	impact	promote	selfish
discourage	influence	prophecy	siblings
discredited	mixed	results	spacing
evidence	nonexistent	rivalry	

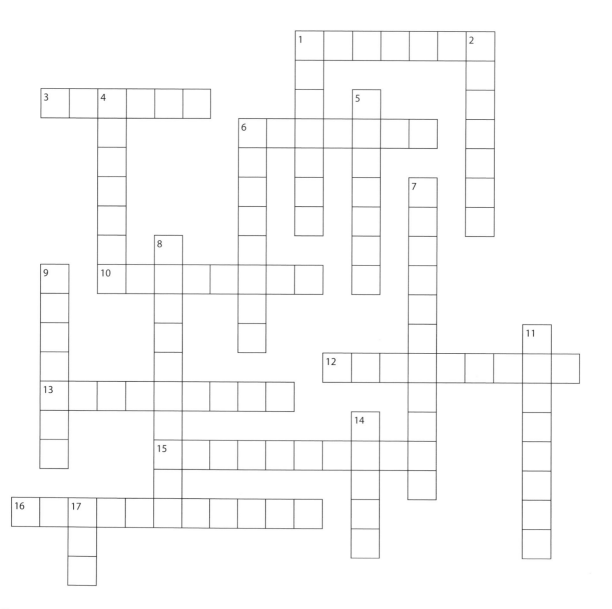

Crossword Puzzle Clues

ACROSS CLUES

1. The _____ of the recent study on birth order are very clear.

3. The _____, or effect, of birth order on people is fun to believe.

6. Many parents plan the _____ of their children so they are born every three years.

10. The scientists Ernst and Angst did not find any _____ for a special personality among the oldest children in a family.

12. The oldest child in a family is called the _____.

13. What factors _____ personality the most as we grow up?

15. The _____ that birth order has a permanent effect on one's personality is not correct.

16. Scientists have _____ earlier research which claimed that all firstborns had a special personality.

DOWN CLUES

1. Fernando has no _____, or competition, between himself and his brothers.

2. Anna is very _____. She only thinks about herself.

4. Most parents _____ achievement among their children. They like to encourage them to do well.

5. Judith Blake believes that the attention of parents is _____, or weakened, when they have many children.

6. Your brothers and sisters are your _____.

7. Research has shown that birth-order differences among children are _____. There is no difference!

8. Parents often _____ their children when they criticize them too much.

9. Parents cannot _____ how their children will be when they grow up.

11. People are often not aware that a self-fulfilling _____ can affect their behavior.

14. Many of the research results are _____ when looking at personality and birth order.

17. _____ is an abbreviation for the Scholastic Aptitude Test.

Prereading

1. Read the title of the chapter, and look at the photo.
  a. How do you think the people in the photo feel about themselves?
  b. What is self-esteem?

2. Work alone. Complete the following chart. How did you feel about yourself at each stage of your life? Was your self-esteem high or low?

Childhood	Adolescence	Young Adulthood	Adulthood

3. Work in a small group. Compare your answers in the chart. Did you all have the same level of self-esteem at the same stages of your lives?

Reading

Highs and Lows in Self-Esteem

by Kim Lamb Gregory, *Scripps Howard News Service*

No one in the Gould family of Westlake Village, California, was surprised by a study suggesting a person's age and stage of life may have a bigger impact on self-esteem than we ever realized. A study of about 350,000 people likens a person's self-esteem across the human lifespan to a roller coaster ride, starting with an inflated

5   sense of self-approval in late childhood that plunges in adolescence. Self-esteem rises steadily through adulthood, only to drop to its lowest point ever in old age. "I've gone through pretty much all of those cycles," Fred Gould said. At 60, he's edging toward retirement. Fred's wife, Eileen, 46, is a businesswoman in the throes of mid-adulthood and, according to the study, predisposed to a healthy self-regard. At 21, the Goulds'

10   son, Jeff, has just launched that heady climb into adulthood and a buoyant self-regard after an adolescence fraught with the usual perils of self-doubt and hormonal warfare.

His sister, Aly, 17, disagrees with a lot of the study, believing instead that each individual has an intrinsic sense of self-esteem that remains relatively constant. But she does agree that adolescence can give even the most solid sense of self-esteem a

15   sound battering. "As a teenager, I can definitely speak for all of us when I say we criticize ourselves," Aly said.

The Study

Demographics

The drop in self-esteem in adolescence was no surprise to Richard Robins, a psychology professor at the University of California at Davis, who spearheaded the study, but "the drop in old age is a little bit more novel," he said. Specifically, Robins was

20   intrigued by the similarities in self-esteem levels between those entering adolescence and old age. "There is an accumulation of losses occurring all at once, both in old age and adolescence," he suggested. "There is a critical mass of transition going on."

Those answering the survey ranged in age from 9 to 90. They participated in the survey by logging onto a website during a period between 1999 and 2000. About

25   three-quarters were Caucasian, the rest a mixture of people of Asian, black, Latino, and Middle Eastern descent. Most were from the United States. The survey simply asked people to agree or strongly disagree—on a five-point scale—with the statement: "I see myself as someone who has high self-esteem."

Everybody is an individual, Robins stressed, so self-esteem can be affected by

30   a number of things that are biological, social, and situational, but there are certain passages that all of us face—and each passage can have a powerful effect on our

sense of self. "With kids, their feelings about themselves are often based on relatively superficial information," Robins explained. "As we get older, we base our self-esteem on actual achievements and feedback from other people."

35 Overall, the study indicated that women do not fare as well as men in self-esteem—a difference particularly marked in adolescence. "During adolescence, girls' self-esteem dropped about twice as much as boys'," Robins said, perhaps at least partially because of society's heavy emphasis on body image for girls. Add one negative life event to all of this turmoil, and a teenager's delicate self-esteem can crumble.

Emerging into Adulthood

40 Eileen remembered having fairly high self-esteem from ages 12 to 16. She had been very ill as a child, so the teen years were a time for her to blossom. Then her mother died when she was 17, and her self-esteem bottomed out. "I was like, 'What do I do? How do I handle this?'" Eileen remembered. Eileen was 22 when she married Fred, an event that coincided with the beginning of her adult years—and an upswing in her self-
45 esteem. Like many adults, Eileen gained her senses of competence and continuity, both of which can contribute to the rise in self-esteem during the adult years, Robins said.

Even if there is divorce or some other form of chaos, there has been a change in our ability to cope, he said. We learn with experience. Fred is aware that his sense of self-esteem may be vulnerable when he retires. "I'm concerned about keeping my
50 awareness level," he said. "Am I going to be aware of the social scene? Of things more global? Am I going to be able to read and keep up with everything?"

Seniors do tend to experience a drop in self-esteem when they get into their 70s, the study says—but not always. This is enigmatic to Robins. "When we look at things like general well-being, the evidence is mixed about what happens in old age," he said.
55 Some people experience a tremendous loss of self-esteem, whereas others maintain their sense of well-being right through old age. Others are not as lucky. Whereas adolescents lose their sense of childhood omnipotence, seniors experience another kind of loss. Retirement comes at about the same time seniors may begin to lose loved ones, their health, their financial status, or their sense of competence. Suddenly,
60 someone who was so in charge may become withdrawn, sullen, and depressed. Their self-esteem may plummet. Robins hopes the study will make us more aware of the times when our self-esteem can be in jeopardy.

Fact Finding

Read the passage again. Then read the following statements. Check (√) whether each statement is True or False. If a statement is false, rewrite it so that it is true. Then go back to the passage and find the line that supports your answer.

1. _____ True _____ False   A person's self-esteem is high during childhood.

_____

2. _____ True _____ False   A person's self-esteem does not change during adolescence.

_____

3. _____ True _____ False   All people experience their lowest self-esteem during old age.

_____

4. _____ True _____ False   The people in the study were mostly Asian.

_____

5. _____ True _____ False   Our self-esteem is affected by several factors.

_____

6. _____ True _____ False   Our self-esteem is most delicate when we are adults.

_____

7. _____ True _____ False   Older people's self-esteem always drops when they get into their 70s.

_____

Reading Analysis

Read each question carefully. Circle the number or letter of the correct answer, or write your answer in the space provided.

1. Read the first paragraph. The author compares the changes in a person's self-esteem over a lifetime to a roller coaster ride. How does the author think a person's self-esteem changes during a lifetime?
    a. It continues to rise throughout the person's life.
    b. It begins high, but it decreases throughout a person's life.
    c. It begins high, then it gets lower and higher throughout a person's life.

2. Read lines 1–3.
    a. **Impact** means
       1. an effect.
       2. a reason.
       3. a result.
    b. **Realized** means
       1. understood.
       2. cared.
       3. remembered.
    c. This sentence means that before the study the Gould family
       1. thought that a person's self-esteem never changed.
       2. understood the connection between age and self-esteem.
       3. didn't understand that a person's self-esteem changes with age.

3. Read lines 3–6.
    a. **Likens** means
       1. enjoys.
       2. compares.
       3. excites.
    b. Which word in these sentences is a synonym for **plunge**?

       _____

    c. These two words mean to
       1. increase.
       2. stay the same.
       3. decrease.

4. Read lines 7–8. **Edging toward** means
   a. becoming sharper.
   b. moving close to.
   c. getting older.

5. In line 10, **launched** means
   a. begun.
   b. finished.
   c. dropped.

6. Read lines 12–16. Aly believes that teenagers
   a. feel good about themselves.
   b. have negative feelings about themselves.
   c. have high self-esteem.

7. Read lines 17–19.
   a. **Spearheaded** means
      1. led.
      2. attacked.
      3. joined.
   b. Robins said that **"the drop in old age is a little bit more novel."** He means that the drop in self-esteem in old age is more
      1. like a book.
      2. unusual.
      3. expected.

8. Read lines 19–22.
   a. Robins was **intrigued** by the similarities in self-esteem between those entering adolescence and old age.
      1. **Intrigued** means
         a. fascinated.
         b. confused.
         c. shocked.
      2. Robins was intrigued because self-esteem is
         a. different in teenagers and in elderly people.
         b. almost the same in teenagers as in elderly people.
         c. the same for people of all ages.
   b. **Accumulation** means
      1. a building up.
      2. a series of.
      3. a number of.

c. **Transition** means
   1. unhappiness.
   2. change.
   3. aging.

9. Read line 23. **Those** refers to
   a. the people who responded to the survey.
   b. the people who wrote the survey.
   c. the people who mailed out the survey.

10. Read lines 29–32, "**. . . there are certain passages that all of us face . . .**" In this sentence, **passages** refers to
   a. trips that we take.
   b. stages in our lives.
   c. places that we visit.

11. Read lines 32–34.
   a. **Superficial information** and **actual achievements** are
      1. opposite ideas.
      2. similar ideas.
   b. **Feedback from other people** means
      1. questions from other people.
      2. decisions by other people.
      3. responses of other people.

12. Read lines 35–36.
   a. **Overall** means
      1. in general.
      2. first.
      3. of course.
   b. **Fare** means
      1. work.
      2. manage.
      3. grow.
   c. These sentences mean
      1. teenage boys and girls have the same level of self-esteem.
      2. teenage boys have lower self-esteem than teenage girls do.
      3. teenage girls have lower self-esteem than teenage boys do.

13. In line 38, **emphasis** means
   a. importance.
   b. unimportance.

14. Read lines 40–43.

    a. **Blossom** means

        1. develop well.

        2. grow flowers.

        3. get taller.

    b. **Bottomed out** means

        1. reached a very high point.

        2. reached a very low point.

        3. changed greatly.

15. Read lines 43–46.

    a. Which word in these sentences is a synonym of **upswing**?

    _____

    b. These two words mean

        1. change.

        2. decrease.

        3. increase.

    c. **Competence** means

        1. job or career.

        2. age or maturity.

        3. skill or ability.

16. Read lines 47–49.

    a. In these sentences, what is an example of **chaos**?

    _____

    b. **Our ability to cope** means we

        1. are able to handle a situation.

        2. are able to change a situation.

        3. are afraid to try something new.

    c. **Vulnerable** describes a situation that is

        1. easy to understand and manageable.

        2. confusing and hard to control.

        3. new and different.

17. Read lines 52–54.

    a. **Enigmatic** means

        1. negative.

        2. puzzling.

        3. optimistic.

b. The evidence is **mixed** means it is
   1. confused.
   2. varied.
   3. combined.

18. Read lines 55–59. Which one of the following statements is true?
    a. Both adolescents and seniors experience the same sense of loss.
    b. Adolescents experience a sense of loss, but seniors do not.
    c. Both adolescents and seniors experience different kinds of loss.

19. Read lines 59–60.
    a. **In charge** means
       1. to have a job.
       2. to retire.
       3. to have control.
    b. The words **withdrawn**, **sullen**, and **depressed** describe a person who is
       1. old.
       2. very unhappy.
       3. excited.
    c. Why do some people become **withdrawn**, **sullen**, and **depressed**?
       1. Because they are no longer in control of their lives.
       2. Because they no longer have jobs.
       3. Because they are older now.

20. In line 62, **in jeopardy** means
    a. in danger.
    b. about to change.
    c. in question.

21. What is the main idea of the passage?
    a. Most people's self-esteem is affected by several factors.
    b. We all face certain passages during our lifetimes.
    c. We all go through passages in life that affect our self-esteem.

Vocabulary Skills

PART 1

Recognizing Word Forms

In English, some verbs change to nouns by adding *-tion* or *-ion*, for example, *collect (v.)*, *collection (n.)*.

Complete each sentence with the correct word on the left. Use the correct form of the verb in either the affirmative or negative. All the nouns are singular.

suggest *(v.)*

suggestion *(n.)*

1. The study at the University of California at Davis _____ that a person's age affects self-esteem. Many people in the study were not surprised by this _____.

participate *(v.)*

participation *(n.)*

2. The people who _____ in the study were between the ages of 9 and 90. The _____ of people of all ages was very important to the results.

accumulate *(v.)*

accumulation *(n.)*

3. Professor Robins believes that teenagers and older people have an _____ of losses. Both adolescents and seniors _____ many losses at the same time.

realize *(v.)*

realization *(n.)*

4. Before the study, Professor Robins _____ the importance of age to self-esteem. The _____ that our self-worth changes over our lifespan was a result of the study.

contribute *(v.)*

contribution *(n.)*

5. As adults, the feeling of competence _____ to high self-esteem. In addition, the ability to manage difficult situations is an important _____ to self-regard as well.

PART 2

Synonyms

Synonyms are words with the same, or similar meaning, for example, *happy, joyful,* and *pleased* are synonyms.

Read each sentence. Write the synonym of the word or phrase in parentheses in the space provided. Use each word only once.

accumulation	enigmatic	self-esteem	unhappy
competence	intrigued	transition	upswing
drop	jeopardy		

1. Kim seems very _____ (*depressed*) since she started her new school. She rarely goes out with her friends and spends most of her time alone in her room.

2. The temperature today is beginning to _____ (*plunge*). It is 20 degrees colder this afternoon than it was this morning.

3. Fatima has not been studying. Her grades will be in _____ (*danger*) if she fails her exams.

4. Children usually have a great sense of _____ (*self-confidence*) when they know that their parents love them and take care of them.

5. It has been snowing all night. There is a two-foot _____ (*buildup*) of snow on the ground.

6. The _____ (*change*) from adolescence to the teen years is often a difficult one, especially for girls.

7. The children have gained considerable _____ (*skill*) at playing baseball because they have been practicing every weekend.

8. Sue was feeling withdrawn and sullen for a while, but her feelings are on the

   _____ (*rise*) now because she likes her new school.

9. We were all _____ (*fascinated*) by the idea of studying abroad for six months.

10. Carlo is a very _____ (*puzzling*) person. He is very hard to know because he is so quiet and unpredictable.

Vocabulary in Context

Read the following sentences. Complete each sentence with the correct word from the box. Use each word only once.

accumulation *(n.)*	emphasis *(n.)*	launch *(v.)*	realize *(v.)*
chaos *(n.)*	feedback *(n.)*	overall *(adv.)*	transition *(n.)*
cope *(v.)*	intrigued *(adj.)*		

1. I wrote an essay in my writing class yesterday. After the instructor gives me

   _____ , I will revise it and improve it.

2. After the earthquake, there was _____ in the city. There was no electricity or clean water, and many people were homeless.

3. For many students, going to college and living away from home is a big _____ in their lives.

4. Carol went to the store early, but it was closed. She didn't _____ that it was Sunday, and the store wouldn't open until 11:00 a.m.

5. Although Miguel's new classes are difficult and he has a lot of homework to do,

   _____ he's very pleased with his new school.

6. Mi Jin and her sister are very successful. Their family puts great _____ on the importance of working hard in order to succeed.

7. Anna was _____ by her new neighbors, so she invited them to her home for dinner to get to know them better.

8. Because Steven and Niko are very lazy and never clean up after dinner, there is a(n)

   _____ of dirty pots and dishes in the sink.

9. Gigi's new business is not very successful. In order to improve it, she will _____ a website for her business very soon.

10. It was difficult for Manuel to _____ at first when he was away from his family. He started to feel much better when he got a job and made new friends.

Reading Skill

Creating a Flowchart

Flowcharts show certain kinds of information, such as cause and effect, and how people come to conclusions. Creating a flowchart can help you organize and understand important information from a reading passage.

Read the article again. The author compares the stages of self-esteem to a roller coaster ride. Write the different stages of a person's self-esteem in the arrows in the chart below. Then write reasons for each stage.

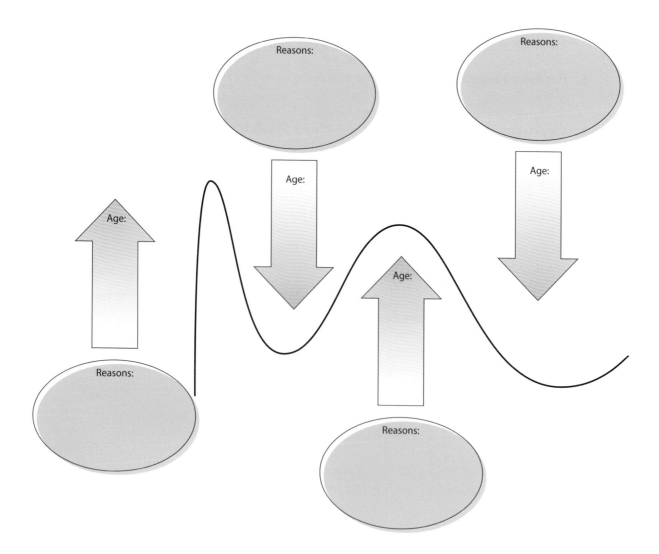

Information Recall

Read each question carefully. Use your flowchart to answer the questions. Do not refer back to the text.

1. What are the different stages of self-esteem that most people go through? Name and briefly describe each one.

   _____

   _____

   _____

   _____

   _____

2. For each stage, what happens in people's lives to cause these changes in self-esteem?

   _____

   _____

   _____

   _____

   _____

Writing a Summary

A summary is a short paragraph that provides the most important information in a reading. It usually does not include details, just main ideas. When you write a summary, it is important to use your own words and not copy directly from the reading.

Write a brief summary of the passage. It should not be more than five sentences. Use your own words. The first two sentences of the summary are below. Write three more sentences to complete the summary.

According to a recent study, our self-esteem rises and drops throughout our lives. However, not everyone agrees with this finding.

Topics for Discussion and Writing

1. What are some ways that adolescents can maintain their sense of self-esteem in spite of the losses they experience? What advice would you give an adolescent who is suffering a drop in self-esteem?

2. According to Richard Robins, self-esteem is affected by biological, social, and situational factors. Work with a partner or in a small group. Discuss which biological, social, and situational factors might affect people at each stage of life. Use the chart below to organize your ideas.

	Childhood	Adolescence	Young Adulthood	Adulthood
Biological Factors				
Social Factors				
Situational Factors				

3. Write in your journal. The author compares the stages of self-esteem in our lives to a roller coaster. Do you think this is an accurate comparison? Why or why not? What analogy would you use to describe your own stages of self-esteem?

Critical Thinking

1. The author states that "There is an accumulation of losses occurring all at once, both in old age and adolescence." (p. 41, lines 21–22) What losses do you think occur at these two stages of our lives? Why do you think so?

2. In terms of self-esteem, adolescent girls do not manage as well as adolescent boys. Why is body image such a focus for girls, as opposed to boys? Is this focus beginning to change for boys? Why or why not?

3. What do you think Professor Richard Robins' opinion is about the results of the self-esteem study discussed in the article? Does he think the findings of the study are important? Why or why not?

Crossword Puzzle

Review the words in the box below. Then read the clues on the next page. Write the words in the correct spaces in the puzzle.

accumulation	fare	launch	plunge
chaos	feedback	liken	realize
competence	impact	novel	spearhead
depressed	intrigued	overall	transition
emphasis	jeopardy	passages	upswing
enigmatic			

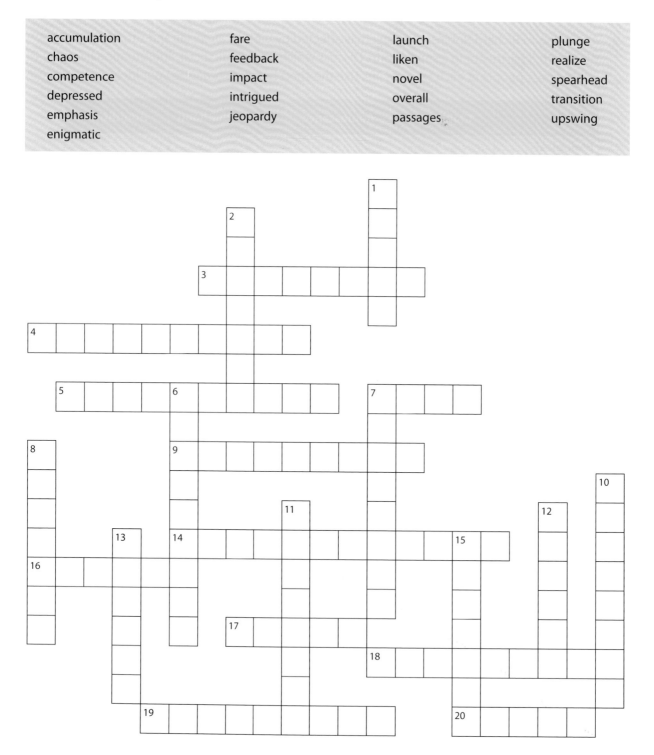

Crossword Puzzle Clues

ACROSS CLUES

3. All humans must experience certain _____ as they move through life.

4. The _____ from childhood to adolescence is often difficult, but not always so.

5. We all need to feel that we have _____, or skills, in order to have positive self-esteem.

7. Adolescent girls do not seem to _____ as well in self-esteem as adolescent boys do.

9. I am _____ by the research on self-esteem. I want to read more about it.

14. There is a(n) _____ of losses in old age, but this occurs when we are young, too.

16. It's often difficult to know the _____, or effect, that life events can have on people.

17. We sometimes experience periods of _____ when a situation is out of our control.

18. Other psychologists plan to _____, or lead, new studies into human development.

19. _____ is similar in meaning to *sullen* or *withdrawn*.

20. We can _____ a person's changes in self-esteem to a roller coaster ride because the ups and downs are so great.

DOWN CLUES

1. Something that is _____ is unusual.

2. We often do not _____ the importance of special events until after they occur.

6. Some people have little trouble adjusting to changes in their lives. Others have considerable difficulty. The reasons why are _____. Who really knows why?

7. Almost everyone appreciates positive _____ from others to feel good about themselves.

8. As adults develop knowledge and skills, they may experience a(n) _____ in self-esteem.

10. When people are unhappy and withdrawn, their well-being is often in _____. They need help.

11. Today, people tend to place more _____ on appearance than on skills or intelligence.

12. _____ means to suddenly drop or decrease.

13. Many young people _____ into adulthood unprepared for the stresses they face.

15. What is the _____, or general, state of your self-esteem?

Health and Wellness

A family hiking to stay fit and healthy

1. What kinds of foods do you eat? Where do these foods come from?

2. What do you do when you don't feel well? What do you do to stay healthy?

3. What role do our lifestyles have in keeping us healthy?

Prereading

1. What do you know about sugar? For example, where does it come from? How is it processed? Is it expensive or inexpensive?

2. When you think of types of food that contain sugar, do you think of these items as healthy or unhealthy? Why?

3. The word *sweet* usually describes something that has a lot of sugar in it. What are some other meanings of *sweet*? What do you think the title of the story means?

Reading

🎧 **Read the passage carefully. Then complete the exercises that follow.**

CD 1
TR 5

Sugar: A Not-So-Sweet Story

by Rich Cohen, *National Geographic*

In the beginning, on the island of New Guinea, where sugarcane was domesticated some 10,000 years ago, people picked cane and ate it raw, chewing a stem until the taste hit their tongue like a starburst. A kind of elixir, a cure for every ailment, an answer for every mood, sugar featured prominently in ancient New Guinean myths.

5   Sugar spread slowly from island to island, finally reaching the Asian mainland around 1000 B.C. By A.D. 500, it was being used in India as a medicine. By 600, it had spread to Persia (now Iran), where rulers entertained guests with a plethora of sweets. When Arab armies conquered the region, they carried away the knowledge and love of sugar.

10 Perhaps the first Europeans to come across sugar were British and French crusaders who went east to fight for the Holy Land.[1] They came home full of visions and stories and memories of sugar. The sugar that reached the West was consumed by the nobility, so rare it was classified as a spice.

Columbus planted the New World's first sugarcane in Hispaniola.[2] As more cane

15 was planted, the price of the product fell. As the price fell, demand increased.

In the mid-17th century, sugar began to change from a luxury spice, like nutmeg and cardamom, to a staple, first for the middle class, then for the poor. Sugar was the oil of its day. In 1700, the average Englishman consumed 4 pounds a year. In 1800, the common man ate 18 pounds of sugar. In 1870, that same sweet-toothed person was

20 eating 47 pounds annually. By 1900, he was up to 100 pounds a year. In that span of 30 years, world production of cane and beet sugar exploded from 2.8 million tons a year to 13 million plus. Today, the average American consumes 77 pounds of added sugar annually, or more than 22 teaspoons of added sugar a day.

"It seems like every time I study an illness and trace a path to the first cause,

25 I find my way back to sugar." Richard Johnson is a nephrologist at the University of Colorado in Denver, Colorado. "Why is it that one-third of adults [worldwide] have high blood pressure, when in 1900, only 5 percent had high blood pressure?" he asked. "Why did 153 million people have diabetes in 1980, and now we're up to

---

[1] This sentence refers to a period during the 11th, 12th, and 13th centuries when European Christians tried to regain control of the Holy Land from Muslim people. The Holy Land is a region in present-day Israel and Palestine that is considered sacred by Christians, Jews, and Muslims.
[2] **Hispaniola** is the name for the Caribbean island that includes Haiti and the Dominican Republic.

CHAPTER 4   Sugar: A Not-So-Sweet Story   61

347 million? Why are more and more Americans obese? Sugar, we believe, is one of
the culprits, if not the major culprit."

Recently, the American Heart Association added its voice to warn against too much added sugar in the diet. But its rationale is that sugar provides calories with no nutritional benefit. According to Johnson and his colleagues, this misses the point. Excessive sugar isn't just empty calories; it's toxic. "It has nothing to do with its calories," says endocrinologist Robert Lustig of the University of California, San Francisco. "Sugar is a poison by itself when consumed at high doses."

Johnson summed up the conventional wisdom this way: Americans are fat because they eat too much and exercise too little. But they eat too much and exercise too little because they're addicted to sugar, which not only makes them fatter but, after the initial sugar rush, also saps their energy, leaving them on the couch. "The reason you're watching TV is not because TV is so good," he said, "but because you have no energy to exercise, because you're eating too much sugar."

The solution? Stop eating so much sugar. When people cut back, many of the ill effects disappear. The trouble is, in today's world it's extremely difficult to avoid sugar, which is one reason for the spike in consumption. Manufacturers use sugar to replace taste in foods reduced in fat so that they seem more healthful, such as fat-free baked goods, which often contain large quantities of added sugar.

It's a worst-case scenario: You sicken unto death not by eating foods you love, but by eating foods you hate—because you don't want to sicken unto death.

Fact Finding

Read the passage again. Then read the following statements. Check (√) whether each statement is True or False. If a statement is false, rewrite it so that it is true. Then go back to the passage and find the line that supports your answer.

1. _____ True _____ False Sugarcane is a native plant of Europe.

   _____

2. _____ True _____ False As people moved across the islands, they brought sugarcane plants with them.

   _____

3. _____ True _____ False At a time in the past, Arab armies conquered the Asian mainland.

   _____

4. _____ True _____ False Europeans first discovered sugar when the British and French went to the island of New Guinea.

   _____

5. _____ True _____ False As the supply of sugarcane increased, the price of sugar increased, too.

   _____

6. _____ True _____ False Eating a lot of sugar has no connection to some of today's health problems.

   _____

7. _____ True _____ False When people reduce their sugar consumption, the negative effects of sugar disappear.

   _____

8. _____ True _____ False Many fat-free foods contain large amounts of added sugar.

   _____

Reading Analysis

Read each question carefully. Circle the letter or the number of the correct answer, or write your answer in the space provided.

1. Read lines 1–4.

    a. "... Sugarcane was **domesticated**" means that people

        1. ate it and used it to sweeten their food.

        2. cultivated it in order to eat it.

        3. discovered it and started to sell it.

    b. **Some 10,000 years ago** means

        1. exactly 10,000 years ago.

        2. more than 10,000 years ago.

        3. about 10,000 years ago.

    c. A **cure** is

        1. a treatment.

        2. a food.

        3. an analysis.

    d. An **ailment** is

        1. a complaint.

        2. an illness.

        3. a mood.

    e. In these sentences, a synonym for **cure** is

        1. elixir.

        2. ailment.

        3. mood.

    f. **Prominently** means

        1. noticeably or greatly.

        2. happily or excitedly.

        3. medically or healthily.

    g. **Myths** are

        1. facts about how plants were domesticated.

        2. true stories that people remember.

        3. untrue stories that people like to believe.

2. Read lines 5–8.

    a. **Mainland** refers to

        1. the part of a country that does not include any islands.

        2. the most important area of a country.

        3. the part of a country where people grow plants.

b. Once sugar reached the Asian mainland, its use changed from that of medicine to sweets in about
   1. 500 years.
   2. 1,000 years.
   3. 1,600 years.

c. **Plethora** means
   1. very expensive kinds.
   2. a very large amount.
   3. a very small amount.

3. Read lines 10–13.
   a. The British and French crusaders who went to the Holy Land
      1. fought to try to bring sugar back to Europe.
      2. tried to plant and grow sugar in the Holy Land.
      3. came across sugar for the first time and brought it to Europe.

   b. **Consumed** means
      1. grown.
      2. eaten.
      3. bought.

   c. The **nobility** refers to
      1. poor people.
      2. all people.
      3. rich people.

   d. **The sugar that reached the West was consumed only by the nobility, so rare it was classified as a spice.** This sentence means that in the West,
      1. sugar was so rare that only the wealthy could afford it.
      2. sugar was so rare that very few people could find it.
      3. sugar was considered a spice and only used in small amounts.

4. Read lines 14–17.
   a. Which of the following sequences is correct?
      1. more cane is planted → prices rise → demand increases
      2. more cane is planted → prices decrease → demand decreases
      3. more cane is planted → prices decrease → demand increases

   b. A food **staple** is
      1. a nutritious food.
      2. a common food.
      3. a delicious food.

   c. Examples of food **staples** are
      1. bread or rice.
      2. cookies or cake.
      3. ice cream or butter.

5. Read lines 17–23.

    a. What is the main idea of this paragraph?

        1. Over the past 300 years, the production of sugar has risen dramatically.

        2. Over the past 300 years, the consumption of sugar has risen dramatically.

        3. Over the past 300 years, the price of sugar has risen dramatically.

    b. A **span** of time is

        1. a very long time.

        2. a very short time.

        3. a period of time.

6. Read lines 24–30.

    a. Who said, "It seems like every time I study an illness and trace a path to the first cause, I find my way back to sugar"?

    _____

    b. What is the answer to the three questions asked in lines 26–29?

    _____

    c. **Trace** means

        1. study.

        2. follow.

        3. understand.

    d. A **culprit** is

        1. a wrongdoer.

        2. a type of disease.

        3. a high-calorie food.

7. Read lines 32–36.

    a. A **rationale** is

        1. a warning about something.

        2. a reason for something.

        3. a description of something.

    b. A food that is only **empty calories**

        1. has no nutritional benefit.

        2. has few or no calories.

        3. is good for your health.

    c. Which word is a synonym for **toxic**?

    _____

    d. **At high doses** means

        1. with other foods.

        2. with empty calories.

        3. in excessive amounts.

e. The American Heart Association and Robert Lustig
   1. agree on the reason for avoiding excessive sugar in the diet.
   2. disagree on the reason for avoiding excessive sugar in the diet.

8. Read lines 37–40.
  a. **Conventional wisdom** refers to
   1. a generally accepted belief.
   2. a cultural tradition.
   3. a medical conclusion.
  b. Which of the following sequences is correct?
   1. become addicted to sugar → eat too much, exercise too little → become fat
   2. eat too much, exercise too little → become fat → become addicted to sugar
  c. Something that **saps** your energy
   1. increases your energy.
   2. lessens your energy.
   3. gives you energy.

9. Read lines 43–45.
  a. **Cut back** means
   1. reduce.
   2. stop.
   3. solve.
  b. A **spike** is
   1. a serious addiction.
   2. a large, sudden increase.
   3. an addition to a food.

10. Read lines 48–49.
  a. A **worst-case scenario** is
   1. the most terrible way to become sick.
   2. the most serious disease one can ever have.
   3. the most serious possible result of a situation.
  b. This sentence means that the worst thing that can happen to you is
   1. to become sick and die from eating foods you enjoy eating, such as food with sugar.
   2. to become sick and die from eating foods you don't enjoy eating, in the hope that you won't become sick.

11. What is the main idea of the passage?
  a. Since its spread worldwide, the production of sugar has increased and its cost has decreased so everyone can buy it.
  b. Since its spread worldwide, the production and consumption of sugar has increased so much that it has become a threat to people's health.
  c. Since its spread worldwide, sugar has been added to every type of fat-free food.

Vocabulary Skills

PART 1

Recognizing Word Forms

In English, the verb and noun forms of some words are the same, for example, *answer (n.)* and *answer (v.).*

Complete each sentence with the correct form of the word on the left. Then circle *(v.)* **if you are using a verb or** *(n.)* **if you are using a noun. Use the correct form of the verb in either the affirmative or the negative. All the nouns are singular.**

cure   **1.** Ten thousand years ago, people believed that sugar was a _____
                                                              (n., v.)

                for many ailments. However, modern medicine has shown that sugar

                _____ illnesses.
                    (n., v.)

demand   **2.** As the cost of sugar decreased, the _____ for it increased.
                                           (n., v.)

                More and more people _____ sugar, and it became popular
                                   (n., v.)

                with the rich and the poor.

spike   **3.** The consumption of sugar by the English _____ from
                                                (n., v.)

                1870 to 1900. One reason for the _____ in sugar
                                        (n., v.)

                consumption is that it became less and less expensive.

spread   **4.** The popularity of sugar _____ from island to island
                                             (n., v.)

                before it reached the mainland of Asia. The _____ of sugar
                                        (n., v.)

                was very slow at first.

taste   **5.** Although many people enjoy the _____ of sugar, it
                                                   (n., v.)

contains empty calories. In other words, although sugar

_____ good, it is not nutritious.
(n., v.)

PART 2

Phrasal Verbs

A phrasal verb is a verb plus a preposition or an adverb. Phrasal verbs have a different meaning from the original verb. *Carry away*, *come across*, *cut back on*, *sum up*, and *warn against* are common phrasal verbs.

First, match each phrasal verb with the correct meaning. Then complete each sentence with the correct phrasal verb. Use the past tense if necessary, and use each phrasal verb only once.

_____ 1. carry away   a. accidentally encounter

_____ 2. come across   b. caution or advise

_____ 3. cut back on   c. conclude or explain

_____ 4. sum up   d. reduce or lower

_____ 5. warn against   e. take with or bring with

1. The French and British crusaders were the first Europeans to _____ sugar in the Holy Land. They had never seen it before.

2. The armies had to return home without sugar, but they _____ the knowledge and love of sugar.

3. The American Heart Association and Dr. Johnson both _____ the danger of eating too much sugar.

4. When people _____ eating sugar, many of their illnesses disappear.

5. Dr. Johnson _____ the problem this way: Americans are fat because they eat too much and exercise too little.

Vocabulary in Context

Read the following sentences. Complete each sentence with the correct word or phrase from the box. Use each word or phrase only once.

consumes *(v.)*	cut back on *(v.)*	rationale *(n.)*	staple *(n.)*
culprit *(n.)*	plethora *(n.)*	span *(n.)*	trace *(v.)*
cure *(n.)*	prominently *(adv.)*		

1. Breakfast cereal is a _____ in our home. Our family eats it every morning.

2. Liz had to _____ her hours at her job because she didn't have enough time to do her homework.

3. My uncle grows a _____ of vegetables in his garden every year. He enjoys the variety of tastes and colors.

4. Olivia _____ too much junk food. It's not healthy for her to eat so many empty calories every day.

5. In the _____ of just five years, Taylor established a very successful business.

6. When our dog ran away last winter, we quickly found him because it was easy to

    _____ his footprints in the snow.

7. The Fleming family is very patriotic. They _____ display the country's flag in front of their home every day.

8. Carlos wanted to go to Europe after he graduated from high school. His _____ was that he wanted to travel for a few years before he started college.

9. Drinking plenty of liquids and getting a lot of rest is the only _____ for the common cold.

10. Our kitchen window was broken yesterday. We found that the _____ was a boy who was playing baseball in the street. He apologized and repaired the window.

Reading Skill

Understanding a Timeline

Timelines show the order of events, such as important dates in history or in a person's life. Using a timeline can help you understand and remember information from a reading passage.

Look at the dates on the timeline. Go back to the reading passage on pages 61–62. Write information about sugar on the timeline in the appropriate place.

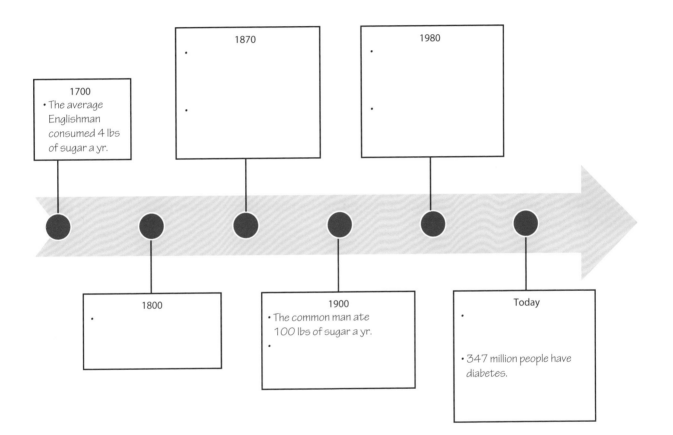

1700
- The average Englishman consumed 4 lbs of sugar a yr.

1870
-

1980
-

1800
-

1900
- The common man ate 100 lbs of sugar a yr.
-

Today
-
- 347 million people have diabetes.

Information Recall

Read the information in the timeline on page 71. Then answer the questions.

1. Which years had the biggest increase in sugar consumption?

_____

2. What was the reason for this?

_____

3. What is a result of the large consumption of sugar?

_____

Writing a Summary

A summary is a short paragraph that provides the most important information in a reading. It usually does not include details, just the main ideas. When you write a summary, it is important to use your own words and not copy directly from the reading.

Write a brief summary of the passage. It should not be more than five sentences. Use your own words. Be sure to indent the first line.

_____

_____

_____

_____

_____

_____

Topics for Discussion and Writing

1. Do people in your culture consume a lot of sugar in their diet? If so, what do you suggest they do to reduce the amount of sugar that they eat? If not, what recommendation can you make to people who need to cut back on sugar consumption?

2. "Manufacturers use sugar to replace taste in foods reduced in fat so that they seem more healthful, such as fat-free baked goods, which often contain large quantities of added sugar." (p. 62, lines 45–47) In other words, manufacturers decrease the fat in some food but increase the sugar. Do you think this makes the food healthier to eat? Why or why not?

3. Write in your journal. Do you think you get enough exercise? Why or why not? What can you do to include more exercise in your daily routine?

Critical Thinking

1. In the beginning, sugar was a luxury used by the nobility. What are some reasons why sugar was first used only by wealthy people? How did it become available to the poor, too? Talk about this with your classmates.

2. According to the article, Dr. Richard Johnson believes that excessive sugar isn't just empty calories; it's toxic. (p. 62, line 33) What does he mean by this? What do you think is his opinion about people who eat too much sugar? Discuss this with your classmates.

3. Go online. Research another plant such as coffee, tea, corn, tomatoes, or potatoes. Find out where that plant originated, what its history is, and how its cultivation spread to areas outside its point of origin. Prepare a speech or PowerPoint presentation to give in class.

Crossword Puzzle

Review the words in the box below. Then read the clues on the next page. Write the words in the correct spaces in the puzzle.

ailment	dose	prominently	staple
consume	elixir	rationale	toxic
culprit	mainland	sap	trace
cure	myth	span	wisdom
domesticated	plethora	spike	

Crossword Puzzle Clues

ACROSS CLUES

2. An example of conventional _____ is "Feed a cold and starve a fever." I don't believe it, though.

6. That drugstore has a(n) _____ of medicines for every illness you can imagine.

7. When sugar became more available and less expensive, there was a huge _____ in the consumption of this item.

8. Many people _____ too much sugar every day. They should eat less sugar.

9. Excessive consumption of sugar can be _____. It is like a poison in large amounts.

10. Researchers can _____ the spread of many crops from their point of origin throughout the world.

12. If you have a bad cold, the best _____ is rest, not medicine.

14. Hawaii is part of the United States, but it is not part of the _____. It is a series of islands.

16. A cold is not a serious _____.

17. I don't understand the _____ behind replacing fat with sugar in food. Sugar isn't healthy in large amounts.

18. In some countries, bread is a(n) _____. In others, it's rice. In others, it's potatoes.

DOWN CLUES

1. Over thousands of years, people _____ many types of plants including wheat, corn, and potatoes.

3. Working long hours and not getting enough sleep can _____ your energy and make you tired.

4. A(n) _____ is a type of remedy for an illness.

5. Stories about the origins of humans, plants, and animals appear _____ in the cultures of many people.

11. Sometimes the _____ in poor health isn't fat—it's an excess of sugar.

13. In a(n) _____ of just 100 years—from 1700 to 1800—the consumption of sugar increased by 350 percent in England.

14. The people of ancient New Guinea had a(n) _____ about the origin of sugar.

15. When you take medicine, be sure to take the proper _____. Do not take too much or too little. Follow the directions.

Prereading

1. What makes you laugh—for example, movies, jokes, funny stories?

2. Are there some actors or comedians that make you laugh? Who are they?

3. Do you like to laugh? How do you feel after you laugh?

4. Do you think laughter is good for your health? Why or why not?

5. Read the title of the article. The title means:
   a. Laughter can always make you feel happy.
   b. You need medicine for your heart.
   c. Laughter may or may not improve your health.

Reading

🎧 **Read the passage carefully. Then complete the exercises that follow.**

Laughter Is the Best Medicine for Your Heart—Or Is It?

The medical community has different views on the effects of laughter on our health. Some research shows that laughter can have health benefits. Other research, however, does not support this idea. This chapter presents two articles with different perspectives on the topic.

The First Perspective: Laughter Is the Best Medicine for Your Heart
by Michelle W. Murray, *University of Maryland Medical Center*

5   Can a laugh every day keep the heart attack away? Maybe so. Laughter, along with an active sense of humor, may help protect you against a heart attack, according to a recent study by cardiologists at the University of Maryland Medical Center in Baltimore. The study, which is the first to indicate that laughter may help prevent heart disease, found that people with heart disease were 40 percent less likely to
10   laugh in a variety of situations compared to people of the same age without heart disease.
    "The old saying that 'laughter is the best medicine' definitely appears to be true when it comes to protecting your heart," says Michael Miller, M.D., director of the Center for Preventive Cardiology at the University of Maryland Medical
15   Center and associate professor of medicine at the University of Maryland School of Medicine. "We don't know yet why laughing protects the heart, but we know that mental stress is associated with impairment of the endothelium, the protective barrier lining our blood vessels. This can cause a series of inflammatory reactions that lead to fat and cholesterol buildup in the coronary arteries and ultimately to a
20   heart attack."
    In the study, researchers compared the humor responses of 300 people. Half of the participants had either suffered a heart attack or undergone coronary artery bypass surgery. The other 150 did not have heart disease. One questionnaire had a series of multiple-choice answers to find out how much or how little people laughed in
25   certain situations, and the second one used true or false answers to measure anger and hostility. Miller said that the most significant study finding was that "people with heart disease responded less humorously to everyday life situations." They

generally laughed less, even in positive situations, and they displayed more anger and hostility.

30   "The ability to laugh—either naturally or as learned behavior—may have important implications in societies such as the United States where heart disease remains the number one killer," says Miller. "We know that exercising, not smoking, and eating foods low in saturated fat will reduce the risk of heart disease. Perhaps regular, hearty laughter should be added to the list."

35   Miller says it may be possible to incorporate laughter into our daily activities, just as we do with other heart-healthy activities, such as taking the stairs instead of the elevator. "We could perhaps read something humorous or watch a funny video and try to find ways to take ourselves less seriously," Miller says. "The recommendation for a healthy heart may one day be exercise, eat right, and laugh a few times a day."

The Second Perspective: Is Laughter the Best Medicine?
by Susan Brink, for *National Geographic*

40   We all want to believe that laughter is good for what ails us, but the science backing that up is thin. However, a few studies relying on laboratory testing do show some benefits.

    "A good belly laugh leads to the release of endorphins from the brain," says Michael Miller, director of the Center for Preventive Cardiology at the University of
45 Maryland Medical Center in Baltimore. That release sets off a cascade of heart-healthy biological events. That leads to the release of nitric oxide, which widens blood vessels, increasing blood flow.

    A study by Miller measured the blood flow of 20 volunteers before and after watching a funny movie and a sad movie. After the sad movie, blood flow was more
50 restricted in 14 of the 20 viewers. But after the movie that made them laugh, average blood flow increased by 22 percent. "The best laugh is one that brings tears to our eyes," says Miller. His prescription: at least 30 minutes of exercise at least three times a week—and 15 minutes of daily laughter.

    Funding for laughter and humor research is low. Mary Bennett, director of the
55 Western Kentucky University School of Nursing, wanted to look into the effect of laughter on the immune system. "It's really hard to get taken seriously when you say you study laughter," she says.

    However, her study of 33 healthy women showed that those who laughed at a humorous movie had higher levels of natural cell activity, which increased their
60 ability to fight off disease. However, the effect was seen only in the subjects who laughed out loud, not in those who quietly watched the comedy.

    Some studies are contradictory. One study of 70 depressed elderly women found that laughter yoga was effective in improving mood. And some studies do show that

a good laugh can help reduce stress hormones. But other studies show that laughter
doesn't affect those hormones.

When Bennett, who has spent much of her career studying laughter and poring over the research literature, is asked whether laughter cures or prevents any disease, her quick answer is a simple "No." Still, she adds, "I think it's a useful addition to real medicine. If you're going through something like chemotherapy, anything you can do to help you stay sane through something that nasty will help."

Fact Finding

Read the passage again. Then read the following statements. Check (√) whether each statement is True or False. If a statement is false, rewrite it so that it is true. Then go back to the passage and find the line that supports your answer.

1. _____ True _____ False   A study at the University of Maryland Medical Center suggests that laughter may protect you from heart disease.

   _____

2. _____ True _____ False   Doctors understand why laughing prevents heart attacks.

   _____

3. _____ True _____ False   All of the people in the study at the University of Maryland Medical Center had heart disease.

   _____

4. _____ True _____ False   According to the study, people with heart disease had more anger and hostility than people without heart disease.

   _____

5. _____ True _____ False   Heart disease is the number one killer in the United States.

   _____

6. _____ True _____ False   Susan Brink believes that there is little scientific support for the belief that laughter improves our health.

   _____

7. _____ True _____ False   Mary Bennett's study showed that women who quietly watched a comedy had increased ability to fight off disease.

   _____

8. _____ True _____ False   Mary Bennett believes that laughter is helpful.

   _____

Reading Analysis

Read each question carefully. Circle the number or letter of the correct answer, or write your answer in the space provided.

1. Read lines 5–11.
   a. **Maybe so** means
      1. maybe by laughing every day, you'll never need medicine for your heart.
      2. maybe laughing every day will help prevent a heart attack.
      3. maybe laughing every day will cause a heart attack.
   b. **Cardiologists** are people who study
      1. heart disease.
      2. laughter.
      3. humor.
   c. The study, which is the first to indicate that laughter may help prevent heart disease, found that people with heart disease were 40 percent less likely to laugh in a variety of situations compared to people of the same age without heart disease.

      This sentence means that people with heart disease
      1. laugh as much as 40 percent of the time in a variety of situations.
      2. laugh 40 percent more often in the same situations than people without heart disease.
      3. do not laugh as much in the same situations as people without heart disease do.
   d. In line 8, **indicate** means
      1. understand.
      2. show.
      3. explain.

2. Read lines 12–20.
   a. **When it comes to** means
      1. with regard to.
      2. at the time of.
      3. at the arrival of.
   b. **Impairment** means
      1. damage.
      2. strengthening.
      3. identification.
   c. What is the **endothelium**?

   _____

   d. How do you know?

   _____

e. **Coronary** refers to
   1. fat.
   2. cholesterol.
   3. the heart.

f. **Ultimately** means
   1. finally.
   2. usually.
   3. quickly.

3. Read lines 21–29.
   a. Who are the **participants**?
      1. The people in the study
      2. The people who had heart attacks
      3. The researchers

   b. How many people in the study had heart disease?

   _____

   c. According to the results of the study, who laughed less?
      1. People without heart disease
      2. People with heart disease
      3. People who were angry

4. Read lines 30–34.
   a. The information between the dashes (—)
      1. provides more information about the kinds of laughter.
      2. explains how laughter affects heart disease.
      3. describes the meaning of laughter in some societies.

   b. **Implications** are
      1. effects.
      2. ideas.
      3. reasons.

   c. How many factors may help reduce the risk of heart disease?
      1. Two
      2. Three
      3. Four

5. Read lines 35–38.
   a. **Incorporate** means
      1. increase.
      2. include.
      3. reduce.

   b. **Humorous** describes something that is
      1. sad.
      2. heart healthy.
      3. funny.

6. Read lines 40–46.

    a. **What ails us** refers to

        1. what makes us sick.

        2. what worries us.

        3. what makes us laugh.

    b. The science **backing** that **up** is thin. **Backing up** means

        1. staying behind.

        2. supporting.

        3. disproving.

    c. **Leads to** means

        1. causes to start.

        2. asks someone to follow.

        3. creates a release.

    d. **Sets off** means

        1. takes away.

        2. releases.

        3. causes.

7. Read lines 49–53.

    a. **Restricted** means

        1. limited.

        2. increased.

        3. active.

    b. A **prescription** is

        1. an idea.

        2. a doctor's instructions.

        3. a direct quote.

8. Read lines 54–61.

    a. **Funding for laughter and humor research is low.** This sentence means that

        1. many people are working on this research.

        2. it's difficult to get money to support this research.

        3. it's important to get money to support this research.

    b. Bennett's study showed that, when watching a humorous movie,

        1. laughing out loud is more beneficial than not laughing.

        2. whether you laugh out loud or not makes no difference.

        3. people only laugh out loud if they think a movie is humorous.

9. Read lines 62–63.

    a. **Contradictory** means

        1. in agreement.

        2. opposing.

        3. confusing.

b. Your **mood** refers to
   1. your health.
   2. your stress.
   3. your feelings.

10. In lines 66–67, **poring over** means
   a. studying something carefully.
   b. learning something new.
   c. writing about something.

11. What is the main idea of the passage?
   a. Cardiologists agree that laughter can protect us against mental stress and heart attacks.
   b. People who have heart disease should laugh for at least 15 minutes every day.
   c. Not everyone agrees that laughter can prevent heart attacks, but most people agree that laughter is good for us.

Vocabulary Skills

PART 1

Recognizing Word Forms

In English, adjectives can change to nouns in several ways. Some adjectives become nouns by adding the suffix -ity, for example, *equal (adj.), equality (n.).*

Complete each sentence with the correct word form on the left. The nouns may be singular or plural.

able *(adj.)*

ability *(n.)*

1. One study showed that women who laughed at a funny movie increased their _____ to prevent diseases. In other words, their immune systems were _____ to fight off illnesses.

active *(adj.)*

activity *(n.)*

2. Some doctors believe that an _____ sense of humor may help protect you against a heart attack. Daily _____, such as watching a funny movie or reading a humorous story, can make us laugh, too.

hostile *(adj.)*   **3.** In his study, Dr. Miller asked questions to measure the participants' anger and

hostility *(n.)*   _____ . He found that people with heart disease laughed less

and were more _____ than people without heart disease.

possible *(adj.)*   **4.** There is a _____ that laughter really is good for our health. As a

possibility *(n.)*   result, Dr. Miller believes it's _____ to include laughter into our

lives every day.

similar *(adj.)*   **5.** Few of the laughter studies had _____ results. There were not

similarity *(n.)*   many _____ in the results of the research discussed in the two

articles.

PART 2

Phrasal Verbs

A phrasal verb is a verb plus a preposition or an adverb. Phrasal verbs have a different meaning from the original verb. *Back up, come to, find out, lead to, rely on, respond to,* and *set off* are common phrasal verbs.

First, match each phrasal verb with the correct meaning. Then complete each sentence with the correct phrasal verb on the left. Use the simple past form of the verb if necessary, and use each phrasal verb only once.

_____ **1.** back up   a. cause

_____ **2.** find out   b. depend on

_____ **3.** lead to   c. discover

_____ **4.** look into   d. investigate

_____ **5.** rely on   e. cause to begin

_____ **6.** respond to   f. react to

_____ **7.** set off   g. support

1. Mary Bennett wanted to _____ the effect of laughter on the immune system, so she read some research to find out if laughter is good for our health.

2. Dr. Miller's research may _____ his idea that laughter can prevent heart attacks. The old saying he quoted is not enough to support his idea.

3. Mental stress can sometimes _____ a buildup of fat and cholesterol in the coronary arteries and ultimately to a heart attack.

4. Dr. Miller found that people with heart disease _____ everyday situations less humorously than people without a history of heart disease.

5. Dr. Miller used a series of multiple-choice answers to _____ how much or how little people laughed in certain situations.

6. Laughter releases endorphins in the brain which _____ heart-healthy actions in our bodies.

7. A lot of research will often _____ laboratory testing for dependable findings.

Vocabulary in Context

Read the following sentences. Complete each sentence with the correct word or phrase from the box. Use each word or phrase only once.

contradictory *(adj.)*	impairment *(n.)*	mood *(n.)*	restricted *(adj.)*
hostile *(adj.)*	implications *(n.)*	pore over *(v.)*	ultimately *(adv.)*
humorous *(adj.)*	incorporate *(v.)*		

1. Voting in the United States is _____. Only people over the age of 18 are permitted to vote. In other words, people under 18 years old cannot vote.

2. Josephine has an important exam next week. She needs to _____ her notes and books this weekend to be sure she is prepared for it.

3. Joe's decision to move across the country has big _____ for his whole family. His wife will need to find a new job, and his children will go to a new school.

4. After Jessica learns English, she wants to go to the university in this city.

   _____, she hopes to get a job here as well.

5. We watched a _____ movie last night. We laughed so hard our stomachs started to hurt!

6. Emelda wants to stay healthy. She thinks it's important to always _____ fresh fruit and vegetables into her diet.

7. I am in a very bad _____ this morning. I overslept, was late for class, and forgot my homework. I hope this day gets better!

8. My brother has a hearing _____ and cannot hear very well. As a result, he always sits in the front of the class so that he can hear the teacher more clearly.

9. The weather reports for today are _____. One reporter said it will rain all day, and another said it's going to be sunny. I'm not sure if I should bring my umbrella to work or not.

10. The clerk at that grocery store is very _____ to the customers. He is never helpful, and he is often rude. I'm going to find a new place to shop for food.

Reading Skill

Organizing Information in a Chart

Organizing information in a chart helps you to better understand what you read. It is especially useful when you want to compare information in two separate readings.

Read the articles again. Underline what you think are the main ideas. Then scan the articles. Fill in the following chart about each article, using the sentences that you have underlined to help you. You will use this chart later to answer specific questions.

	Laughter Is the Best Medicine for Your Heart	Is Laughter the Best Medicine?
Who performed the study?		
Why did they do the study?		
Where did they do the study?		
Who did they study?		
How did they study them?		
What were the results of the study?		
What were the recommendations?		

Information Recall

Read each question carefully. Use the chart to answer the questions. Do not refer back to the text.

1. What do some doctors believe about laughter?

_____

_____

2. Who did Dr. Miller study?

_____

_____

3. What did the researchers learn from Dr. Miller's study?

_____

_____

4. Who did Mary Bennett study?

_____

_____

5. How were her results and Dr. Miller's results different?

_____

_____

Writing a Summary

A summary is a short paragraph that provides the most important information in a reading. It usually does not include details, just main ideas. When you write a summary, it is important to use your own words and not copy directly from the reading.

Write a brief summary of the passage. It should not be more than five sentences. Use your own words. Be sure to indent the first line.

Topics for Discussion and Writing

1. Do you think that the ability to laugh is a natural behavior or a learned behavior? In other words, is the ability to laugh innate, such as the ability to sing, or is it something we can learn to do? Explain your answer.

2. Describe a funny movie that you have seen. What was the name of the movie? What was funny about the movie?

3. Write in your journal. Describe an incident or a story that you think is humorous—something that made you laugh.

Critical Thinking

1. Many doctors believe that mental stress may cause heart disease. Why do you think laughter helps prevent heart disease?

2. According to the article, Mary Bennett, director of the Western Kentucky University School of Nursing, wanted to look into the effect of humor on the immune system, but states that funding for laughter and humor research is low. How does she think the American medical community views laughter in regard to health? Do you think Mary Bennett was able to conduct the study?

3. Is humor culturally determined? In other words, does what we think of as funny depend on the culture we grew up in? Do people from the same culture think that the same things are funny?

4. Take a survey among the class. Does laughing alone make you feel better? Does laughing in a group make you feel better?

Crossword Puzzle

Review the words in the box below. Then read the clues on the next page. Write the words in the correct spaces in the puzzle.

ails	funding	incorporate	pore
cardiologists	humorous	indicate	prescription
coronary	impairment	mood	restricted
endothelium	implication	participants	ultimately

Crossword Puzzle Clues

ACROSS CLUES

4. I prefer _____ movies to serious movies. I like films that are funny.

5. We need to _____ joy and laughter into our everyday lives.

6. _____ means damage, for example, damage to the endothelium.

10. I have to _____ over this research so I can write a paper about it. I need to study it carefully.

11. _____ are doctors who specialize in studying the heart.

12. Laughter can be a wonderful way to help cure what _____ us. People often feel better after laughing.

13. The buildup of fat and cholesterol in our arteries can _____ lead to a heart attack.

14. It can be very difficult to get _____ to study laughter. Few people want to provide money for this research.

15. If you are usually in a good _____, you feel better about yourself and the world around you.

DOWN CLUES

1. Some studies _____ that laughter benefits our health, but other studies do not support that idea.

2. I think that laughter is a very good _____ for health, and it's free!

3. The _____ in a study on heart disease are usually in two groups: one group has heart disease while the other does not.

6. Research that demonstrates the benefits of laughter has an important _____ for our health and well-being.

7. The _____ is the protective barrier that lines our blood vessels.

8. When your blood flow is _____, it does not flow as well as it should through your bloodstream.

9. _____ diseases are diseases of the heart.

Traditional Medicine: A Non-Western Approach to Healing

Native American healer burns sage as part of a healing ritual

Woman gets medicine in a traditional Chinese pharmacy

Prereading

1. What are some differences between modern medicine and traditional medicine? Work with a partner to make a list.

Modern Medicine	Traditional Medicine

2. Which approach to medicine is more effective? Or are they the same? What do you think?

3. Read the title of this article, and look at the photos.
   a. What is the Native American woman doing?
   b. What is the Asian man doing?
   c. What are the activities in these photos examples of?

Reading

Read the passage carefully. Then complete the exercises that follow.

CD 1
TR 7

Traditional Medicine: A Non-Western Approach to Healing

In the twenty-first century, many people rely on what is referred to as Western medicine to heal injuries and illnesses. Western medicine is based on a scientific approach to healing. However, many cultures have different views on healing, and their "medicine ways" are based on these beliefs. Their practices go back hundreds,
5   or even thousands, of years. This chapter describes traditional healing in Native American and Chinese cultures.

Native American Medicine Ways: Underlying Concepts
National Library of Congress

Many traditional healers say that most of the healing is done by the patient and that every person has a responsibility for his or her proper behavior and health. This is a serious, lifelong responsibility. Healers serve as facilitators and counselors to help
10   patients heal themselves. Healers use stories, humor, music, smudging,[1] and ceremonies to bring healing energies into the healing space and focus their effects. The healing process also goes beyond the individual patient. Traditional healers take into account not only the patient's immediate family and community, but future generations as well.

The Key Role of Ceremony

Ceremony is an essential part of traditional Native American healing. Because
15   physical and spiritual health are intimately connected, body and spirit must heal together. Traditional healing ceremonies promote wellness by reflecting Native American concepts of Spirit, Creator, and the Universe. They can include prayer, chants, drumming, songs, and stories.

The Medicine Wheel and the Four Directions

The Medicine Wheel, sometimes known as the Sacred Hoop, has been used by
20   generations of various Native American tribes for health and healing. It embodies the Four Directions, as well as Father Sky, Mother Earth, and Spirit Tree—all of which symbolize dimensions of health and the cycles of life.

Movement in the Medicine Wheel is circular, and typically in a clockwise, or "sun-wise" direction. This helps to align with the forces of Nature, such as the rising and setting of the

---

[1] **Smudging** is a traditional Native American method of burning sacred herbs, such as sage, to produce a smoke cloud which is used in various cleansing or prayer ceremonies and purification or healing rituals.

CHAPTER 6   Traditional Medicine: A Non-Western Approach to Healing   **93**

25 sun. Each of the Four Directions (East, South, West, and North) is typically represented by a distinctive color, such as black, red, yellow, and white. The Directions can also represent the stages of life or the elements of nature—fire (or sun), air, water, and earth.

Healing Plants

Native American healers have a long history of using indigenous, or native, plants for a wide variety of medicinal purposes. They are used to treat many common
30 illnesses, chronic conditions, and injuries, as well as to enhance the immune system. Some examples of native plants and their medicinal properties are the coneflower, bitterroot, and the dandelion.

The roots and seed heads of the purple coneflower are chewed to relieve toothaches, sore throats, and other ailments. A strong tea is made from the root and
35 used to strengthen the immune system and relieve flu and cold symptoms. A strong tea from a root called bitterroot is taken for fever, sore throats, coughs, stomach problems, heart disease, high blood pressure, and diabetes.

The dandelion, which many Westerners consider a weed, or unwanted plant, is actually a generous source of vitamins A, B, C, and D and various minerals. It is also
40 used to treat liver problems.

Chinese Medicine Ways: Underlying Concepts
National Institutes of Health

Traditional Chinese medicine (TCM) originated in ancient China and has evolved over thousands of years. TCM practitioners use herbal medicines and various mind and body practices such as acupuncture[2] and tai chi[3] to treat or prevent health problems. Some of the ancient beliefs on which traditional Chinese medicine is
45 based include the view that the human body is a miniature version of the larger, surrounding universe. Harmony between two opposing yet complementary forces, called *yin* and *yang*, supports health. Disease results from an imbalance between these two forces. Important, too, is the concept of *qi*, a vital energy that flows through the body. *Qi* performs multiple functions in maintaining health.

The Five Elements

50 TCM is also based on the concept that five elements—fire, earth, wood, metal, and water—symbolically represent all phenomena, including the stages of human life. Each element is associated with a specific color and with specific organs of the body. Through viewing the human body in this way, internal disharmony can be determined. For example, if a patient has a green hue to his complexion, a traditional Chinese practitioner
55 would look more closely at the wood element, which involves the liver. Fire is red and connected with the heart. Earth is yellow and is associated with the stomach. The element metal is white and relates to the lungs. Water is black and is associated with the kidneys.

---

[2] **Acupuncture** is a procedure involving the stimulation of specific points on the body. During acupuncture, the skin is penetrated with very thin, metal needles.
[3] **Tai chi** is a mind and body practice involving gentle, dancelike body movements with mental focus, breathing, and relaxation.

Healing Plants

Like the Native American healers, traditional Chinese practitioners have used indigenous plants for the same wide range of medicinal purposes. The Chinese *Materia Medica* (a pharmacological reference book used by TCM practitioners) describes thousands of plants. Different parts of plants, such as the leaves, roots, stems, flowers, and seeds, are used. Some examples of plants that are used in traditional Chinese medicine are cinnamon, ginger, and the flower peony.

According to traditional Chinese medicine, cinnamon encourages circulation, warms the body, balances the energy of the upper and lower body, and reduces allergic reactions. Practitioners use ginger to benefit digestion, increase air to the lungs, warm circulation in the limbs, and treat coughs. The root of the peony is believed to relax the blood vessels, nourish the blood, and promote circulation to the skin and extremities.

Native American and Chinese traditional medicines have many similarities and differences in their underlying concepts, the plants they use, and in several other ways as well, such as the role of ceremony. However, the Native Americans and Chinese who rely on their traditional healing practices believe that they help to heal, and perhaps it is this belief that has made these traditions such an integral part of their cultures for so many centuries.

Fact Finding

Read the passage again. Then read the following statements. Check (√) whether each statement is True or False. If a statement is false, rewrite it so that it is true. Then go back to the passage and find the line that supports your answer.

1. _____ True _____ False   Traditional medicine and Western medicine have different approaches to health and healing.

_____

2. _____ True _____ False   In Native American views, the doctor is responsible for the patient's health.

_____

3. _____ True _____ False   In Native American tradition, the patients, their families, and their communities are all important in the healing process.

_____

4. _____ True _____ False   The Four Directions only represent East, South, West, and North.

_____

5. _____ True _____ False   Native Americans use native plants to heal illnesses and strengthen the immune system.

_____

6. _____ True _____ False   Traditional Chinese medicine treats the mind and body at the same time.

_____

7. _____ True _____ False   According to traditional Chinese medicine, disease is caused by forces outside the body.

_____

8. _____ True _____ False   Traditional Chinese medicine is based on all the same elements as Native American medicine.

_____

Reading Analysis

Read each question carefully. Circle the number or letter of the correct answer, or write your answer in the space provided.

1. Read lines 4–5. **Go back** means
   a. has existed for.
   b. has returned to.
   c. has turned around.

2. Read lines 9–13.
   a. **Facilitators** are people who
      1. have a lifelong responsibility.
      2. help to make something happen.
      3. make patients take care of themselves.
   b. What is **smudging**?

   _____

   c. Where did you find this information?

   _____

   d. This type of information is called
      1. a footnote.
      2. an index.
      3. a preface.
   e. **Ceremonies** are
      1. old stories.
      2. formal practices.
      3. religious songs.
   f. **Energies** means
      1. activities.
      2. treatments.
      3. powers.
   g. **Take into account** means
      1. add up.
      2. consider.
      3. bring with.

3. Read lines 14–18.
   a. **Essential** means
      1. necessary.
      2. happy.
      3. colorful.
   b. **Promote** means
      1. reduce.
      2. encourage.
      3. discuss.
   c. **Concepts** refers to
      1. ceremonies.
      2. stories.
      3. understandings.
   d. In line 17, **they** refers to
      1. Native Americans.
      2. traditional healing ceremonies.
      3. Native American ideas.

4. Read lines 19–22.
   a. **Embodies** means
      1. represents.
      2. directs.
      3. uses.
   b. Which word in these lines is a synonym for **embody**?

   _____

   c. What does the Medicine Wheel, or Sacred Hoop, symbolize? Check (√) all that apply.
      _____ 1. The Spirit
      _____ 2. The Four Directions
      _____ 3. Mother Earth
      _____ 4. The Universe
      _____ 5. Father Sky
      _____ 6. Medicinal plants
      _____ 7. Spirit Tree

   d. The **cycles of life** refer to
      1. the stages of life.
      2. the seasons of the year.
      3. the directions.

5. Read lines 23–26.

   a. A circular, clockwise, or **sun-wise direction** moves in the same direction as

      1. the hands on a clock.

      2. the sun in the sky.

      3. both 1 and 2.

   b. **Align with** means

      1. be in proper position with.

      2. agree with.

      3. go up and down with.

   c. **Distinctive** means

      1. typical.

      2. bright.

      3. special.

6. Read lines 28–34.

   a. **Indigenous plants** are plants that

      1. can heal.

      2. are native to the area.

      3. are used for medicine.

   b. **Chronic** means

      1. habitual; persistent.

      2. serious; dangerous.

      3. common; usual.

   c. **Enhance** means

      1. cure.

      2. examine.

      3. strengthen.

   d. **Ailments** are

      1. illnesses.

      2. injuries.

      3. strong pains.

7. Read lines 41–49.

   a. **Traditional Chinese medicine (TCM) originated in ancient China and has evolved over thousands of years.** This sentence means

      1. TCM began in China thousands of years ago, and it has changed over time.

      2. TCM began in China thousands of years ago, but it has not changed over time.

      3. TCM began so long ago that no one knows its origins, but it is very old.

   b. **Harmony** refers to

      1. calm and balance.

      2. disagreement and opposition.

      3. plants and herbs.

c. **Harmony between two opposing yet complementary forces, called *yin* and *yang*, supports health. Disease results from an imbalance between these two forces.**

These sentences mean that people are healthy when the interdependent forces of *yin* and *yang*

1. are equal.
2. oppose each other.

d. What do traditional Chinese medical practitioners use? Check (√) all that apply.

___ 1. Songs and stories   ___ 4. Mind and body practices
___ 2. Herbal medicines   ___ 5. Special ceremonies
___ 3. Forces of nature   ___ 6. Acupuncture and tai chi

e. What is **qi**?

_____

8. Read lines 50–57.

a. **Phenomena** are
1. the five elements.
2. interesting images or events.
3. the stages of human life.

b. **Internal disharmony** refers to
1. an imbalance inside of the body.
2. a problem with traditional medicine.
3. an illness or a sickness.

c. The sentences in lines 52–55 mean that the changing color of a person's skin
1. reflects the person's stage of life.
2. indicates the part of the body that is ill.
3. shows that the person will become ill.

9. Read lines 69–74.

a. **Underlying** means
1. basic; fundamental.
2. proven to be true; factual.
3. very old; ancient.

b. **Rely on** means
1. care about.
2. be used to.
3. depend on.

c. **Integral** means
1. cultural.
2. essential.
3. ceremonial.

10. What is the main idea of the passage?
   a. Traditional medicine is better for healing illnesses than Western medicine.
   b. Traditional Chinese and Native American medicine, though different, are essential parts of each culture.
   c. Traditional Chinese and Native American medicine go back thousands of years.

Vocabulary Skills

PART 1

Recognizing Word Forms

In English, some nouns become adjectives by adding the suffix -al, for example, *accident (n.)*, *accidental (adj.)*.

Complete each sentence with the correct word form on the left. The nouns may be singular or plural.

tradition *(n.)*

traditional *(adj.)*

1. Chinese medicine is a _____ that goes back thousands of years. The _____ healers believe that all people are responsible for their own health.

ceremony *(n.)*

ceremonial *(adj.)*

2. In the Native American culture, _____ healing promotes wellness. Healers use stories, music, and various _____ to bring healing energies together.

medicine *(n.)*

medicinal *(adj.)*

3. Traditional _____ often uses plants to heal and prevent illness. The healers believe that these plants have _____ qualities.

spirit *(n.)*

spiritual *(adj.)*

4. Native Americans believe that physical health and _____ health are connected. As a result, body and _____ must heal together.

herb *(n.)*

herbal *(adj.)*

5. Both traditional Chinese medicine and Native American practitioners use

_____ medicine in different ways. The Native Americans burn

some _____ to produce a smoke cloud.

PART 2

Using a Dictionary

In English, words may have more than one meaning depending on the context. For example, the verb *change* may refer to exchanging currency. *(Tom changed $300 to euros before going to France.)* It may also mean to become something different. *(Marta changed her life by getting a new job that she enjoys.)* It can mean to switch something for something else. *(My sister went back to the store to change a small handbag for a larger handbag.)*

1. Read the following sentences. Use the context to help you understand the word in bold. Then read the dictionary entry for **practice**, and circle the appropriate definition.

> Many cultures have different views on healing, and their "medicine ways" are based on these beliefs. Their **practices** go back hundreds, or even thousands, of years.

> **practice** /ˈpræktɪs/ *n.* **1** [U] regular repetition of an activity, art, sport, etc.: *It takes practice to do almost anything well.* **2** [C] *usu. sing.* a meeting for this purpose: *The school band has practice at 8 A.M., before classes start.* **3** [U] s.t. that is done regularly, the usual way of doing s.t.: *It is standard business practice to keep a copy of every letter sent out.*‖*He made a practice of always telling the truth.* **4** [U] the carrying out of s.t. in a real situation, actual performance: *The method worked in theory but not in practice.*

2. Circle the number of the sentence that has the appropriate meaning of **practices**.
   a. Their regular repetitions of healing activities go back hundreds, or even thousands, of years.
   b. Their meetings for the purpose of healing go back hundreds, or even thousands, of years.
   c. Their usual ways of healing go back hundreds, or even thousands, of years.
   d. Their actual performances in healing go back hundreds, or even thousands, of years.

3. **Practices** means
   a. rehearsals.
   b. customs.
   c. policies.

4. Read the following sentence. Use the context to help you understand the word in bold. Then read the dictionary entry for **property**, and circle the appropriate definition.

> Some examples of native plants and their medicinal **properties** are the coneflower, bitterroot, and the dandelion.

> **property** /'prɑpərti/ *n.* [C;U] **-ties 1** physical objects owned by s.o.: *His personal property consists of clothes, a wallet, and a watch.* **2** land and buildings, real estate: *She owns property in California.* **3** a characteristic, trait: *Chemicals have certain properties, like cleaners that dissolve grease.*

5. Circle the letter of the sentence that has the appropriate meaning of **properties**.
   a. Some examples of native plants and their medicinal physical objects are the coneflower, bitterroot, and the dandelion.
   b. Some examples of native plants and their medicinal lands are the coneflower, bitterroot, and the dandelion.
   c. Some examples of native plants and their medicinal characteristics are the coneflower, bitterroot, and the dandelion.

6. **Properties** means
   a. traits.
   b. possessions.
   c. territories.

Vocabulary in Context

Read the following sentences. Complete each sentence with the correct word or phrase from the box. Use each word or phrase only once.

ailments *(n.)*	distinctive *(adj.)*	indigenous *(adj.)*	promote *(v.)*
align *(v.)*	enhances *(v.)*	integral *(adj.)*	rely on *(v.)*
chronic *(adj.)*	goes back *(v.)*		

1. My friendship with Denise _____ a very long time. We've been friends since elementary school.

2. A lunar eclipse occurs when the sun, earth, and moon _____ closely, with the earth in the middle.

3. Smartphones and tablets are a(n) _____ part of life in the 21st century.

4. Andrés has _____ back pain because he sits at his computer all day. His doctor advised him to exercise to relieve the pain.

5. Some women wear makeup because they believe that it _____ their appearance.

6. Most colleges in the United States prohibit cigarette smoking on campus in order to _____ a healthy environment for students.

7. Children _____ their parents completely when they are young, but they become more independent as they grow up.

8. My puppy has _____ markings on his coat. He looks very different from most other dogs.

9. There are several Native American tribes that are _____ to this part of the United States.

10. Common _____, such as mild coughs and colds, can usually be treated without the help of a doctor.

Reading Skill

Using a Venn Diagram

Venn diagrams show the differences and similarities between two topics. Using a Venn diagram can help you organize and understand important information from a reading passage.

Read the passage again, and then read the sentences below. Write the sentences in the correct place in the Venn diagram.

- ~~Illnesses are caused by an imbalance between two forces.~~
- Ceremony is an essential part of traditional healing.
- It uses indigenous plants for medical purposes.
- Elements such as fire and water are symbolic.
- The healing process includes the patient, his or her family, and the community.
- Elements are associated with specific organs of the body.
- The patient is responsible for his or her own health.

- Views on healing practices go back many centuries.
- The human body is a miniature version of the universe.

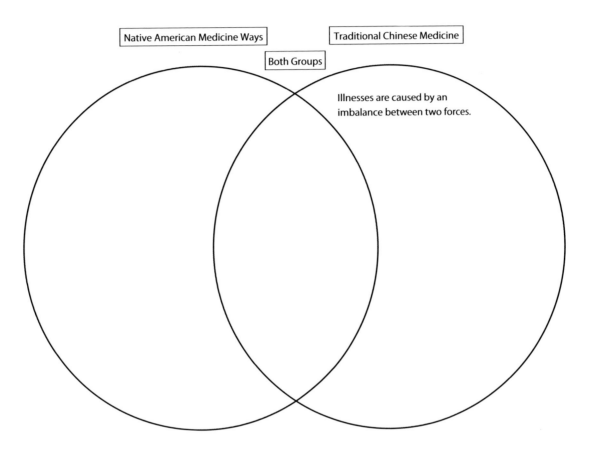

Native American Medicine Ways

Both Groups

Traditional Chinese Medicine

Illnesses are caused by an imbalance between two forces.

Information Recall

Read the passage again, and review the Venn diagram. Then answer the questions.

1. How are Native American medicine ways and traditional Chinese medicine ways similar?

_____

_____

2. How are they different?

_____

_____

Writing a Summary

A summary is a short paragraph that provides the most important information in a reading. It usually does not include details, just main ideas. When you write a summary, it is important to use your own words and not copy directly from the reading.

Write a brief summary of the passage. It should not be more than five sentences. Use your own words. Be sure to indent the first line.

Topics for Discussion and Writing

1. Do you know of another kind of traditional medicine? What is it? What is it used for? Discuss this with your classmates.

2. Have you or someone you know ever used any of the traditional medicine described in this chapter? Tell your classmates about it. Do you think it was helpful? Why or why not?

3. Write in your journal. What do you do to keep yourself well or heal yourself when you are sick? Do you rely on a traditional type of medicine, for example?

Critical Thinking

1. Traditional medicine is still used in many cultures today instead of Western medicine. What do you think are some reasons for this? Discuss it with your classmates.

2. Can traditional ways of healing work side by side with modern methods of healing? Why or why not?

3. In the last sentence of the article, the author states, "However, the Native Americans and Chinese who rely on their traditional healing practices believe that they help to heal, and perhaps it is this belief that has made these traditions such an integral part of their cultures for so many centuries." What do you think is the author's opinion of the power of the mind? Why does he think the traditional healing practices are effective?

Preparing medicine in a traditional Chinese pharmacy

Crossword Puzzle

Review the words in the box below. Then read the clues on the next page. Write the words in the correct spaces in the puzzle.

ailments	disharmony	essential	internal
align	distinctive	facilitator	phenomena
ceremonies	embodies	healers	promotes
chronic	energies	indigenous	smudging
cycles	enhance	integral	underlying

Crossword Puzzle Clues

ACROSS CLUES

4. Native American medicine _____ wellness through a range of rituals.

5. Non-traditional medicine has cures for many _____, or illnesses.

7. Native Americans have many traditional _____, including singing religious songs and telling old stories.

10. There are many _____, or fundamental, concepts behind traditional medicine.

12. Both Native Americans and the Chinese use _____, or native, plants in their practices.

16. In Native American medicine, the patient cures himself or herself. The person who works with him or her is a(n) _____ in the process but does not actually cure the person.

17. _____ refers to burning sacred herbs to create smoke as part of some rituals.

18. In traditional Chinese medicine, external appearance is an indicator of _____ imbalances.

19. Stories and music bring special _____ into the process of curing a patient.

20. Medicinal plants are used to _____, or strengthen, the immune system.

DOWN CLUES

1. Traditional medicine treats _____, or persistent, illnesses.

2. The people who are trained in Native American medicine ways are called _____.

3. The five elements symbolically represent all _____, including stages of life.

6. Moving in the direction of the Medicine Wheel helps to _____ with the forces of nature.

8. In Native American tradition, the Four Directions are each represented by a(n) _____ color, one for each direction.

9. Traditions have been a(n) _____ part of traditional medicine for many centuries.

11. In traditional Chinese medicine, illness is often connected with _____, or imbalances in the body.

13. The Medicine Wheel _____, or represents, the Four Directions.

14. There are several _____, or stages, of life from birth to death.

15. Rituals are a(n) _____ part of traditional Native American medicine.

Science and Technology

Scientists at MIT's CityFARM founded by National Geographic Explorer Caleb Harper studying plants in a farm laboratory

1. When we are sick, what types of drugs should we take? Should we take drugs often? Why or why not?

2. Are some animals more intelligent than others? What can we learn from animals?

3. What kinds of sciences are interesting to you? Why are they interesting?

Prereading

1. What are bacteria?
   a. Microorganisms that are not really alive
   b. Microscopic living organisms
   c. Very small animals

2. What can bacteria do? Check (√) all that apply.
   _____ a. Cause diseases   _____ c. Cause infections
   _____ b. Fight infections   _____ d. Help digest food

3. Read the title of this article. What are *superbugs*?
   a. A very common kind of bacteria that everyone has
   b. A very dangerous kind of bacteria that is difficult to stop
   c. A kind of bacteria that grows quickly

4. The title means
   a. we need to stop insects from multiplying.
   b. we need to stop harmful bacteria from spreading.
   c. we need to stop bugs from becoming larger.

Reading

🎧 Read the passage carefully. Then complete the exercises that follow.

CD 2
TR 1

Stopping the Spread of Superbugs
National Institutes of Health

For nearly a century, bacteria-fighting drugs known as antibiotics have helped to control and destroy many of the harmful bacteria that can make us sick. But in recent decades, antibiotics have been losing their punch against some types of bacteria. In fact, certain bacteria are now unbeatable with today's medicines. Sadly, the way we've
5   been using antibiotics is helping to create new drug-resistant "superbugs."

Superbugs are strains of bacteria that are resistant to several types of antibiotics. Each year these drug-resistant bacteria infect more than two million people nationwide and kill at least 23,000, according to the U.S. Centers for Disease Control and Prevention (CDC).

Antibiotics are among the most commonly prescribed drugs for people.
10 Antibiotics are effective against bacterial infections, such as strep throat, some types of pneumonia, eye infections, and ear infections. But these drugs don't work at all against viruses,[1] such as those that cause colds or flu.

Unfortunately, many antibiotics prescribed to people and to animals are unnecessary. Furthermore, the overuse and misuse of antibiotics help to create drug-
15 resistant bacteria. Here's how that might happen. When used properly, antibiotics can help destroy disease-causing bacteria. However, if you take an antibiotic when you have a viral infection like the flu, the drug won't affect the viruses making you sick. Instead, it'll destroy a wide variety of bacteria in your body, including some of the "good" bacteria that help you digest food, fight infection, and stay healthy. Bacteria
20 that are tough enough to survive the drug will have a chance to grow and quickly multiply. These drug-resistant strains may even spread to other people.

Over time, if more and more people take antibiotics when not necessary, drug-resistant bacteria can continue to thrive and spread. They may even share their drug-resistant traits with other bacteria. Drugs may become less effective or not work at all
25 against certain disease-causing bacteria. Scientists have been trying to keep ahead of newly emerging drug-resistant bacteria by developing new drugs, but it's a tough task.

You can help slow the spread of drug-resistant bacteria by taking antibiotics properly and only when needed. Don't insist on an antibiotic if your health care provider advises otherwise. For example, many parents expect doctors to prescribe
30 antibiotics for a child's ear infection. But experts recommend delaying for a time in certain situations, as children often recover from ear infections without antibiotics.

---

[1] **Viruses** are microorganisms that cannot grow or reproduce apart from a living cell.

NIH[2] researchers have been looking at whether antibiotics are effective for treating certain conditions in the first place. One recent study showed that antibiotics may be less effective than previously thought for treating a common type of sinus infection.

35 This kind of research can help prevent the misuse and overuse of antibiotics. "Treating infections with antibiotics is something we want to preserve for generations to come, so we shouldn't misuse them," says Dr. Julie Segre, a senior investigator at NIH.

In the past, some of the most dangerous superbugs have been confined to health care settings. That's because people who are sick or in a weakened state are more susceptible

40 to picking up infections. But superbug infections aren't limited to hospitals. Some strains are out in the community and anyone, even healthy people, can become infected.

One common superbug increasingly seen outside hospitals is methicillin-resistant *Staphylococcus aureus* (MRSA). These bacteria don't respond to methicillin[3] and related antibiotics. MRSA can cause skin infections and, in more serious cases, pneumonia or

45 bloodstream infections.

"We rely on antibiotics to deliver modern health care," Segre says. But with the rise of drug-resistant bacteria, "we're running out of new antibiotics to treat bacterial infections," and some of the more potent ones aren't working as well. Ideally, doctors would be able to quickly identify the right antibiotic to treat a particular infection.

50 But labs need days or even weeks to test and identify the bacteria strain. Until the lab results come in, antibiotic treatment is often an educated guess. While scientists search for ways to beat back these stubborn bacteria, you can help by preventing the spread of germs so we depend less on antibiotics in the first place.

The best way to prevent bacterial infections is by washing your hands frequently

55 with soap and water. It's also a good idea not to share personal items such as towels or razors. And use antibiotics only as directed. We can all do our part to fight drug-resistant bacteria.

---

[2] **NIH** is the National Institutes of Health.
[3] **Methicillin** is a type of antibiotic. It is rarely used now because staph bacteria have become resistant to it.

A common type of bacteria

Fact Finding

Read the passage again. Then read the following statements. Check (√) whether each statement is True or False. If a statement is false, rewrite it so that it is true. Then go back to the passage and find the line that supports your answer.

1. _____ True _____ False   Superbugs cannot always be killed with today's medicines.
_____

2. _____ True _____ False   Sometimes people use antibiotics when they do not need them.
_____

3. _____ True _____ False   Bacteria that are not affected by some drugs continue to live and to spread.
_____

4. _____ True _____ False   It is always advisable to use a drug as soon as an infection appears.
_____

5. _____ True _____ False   Bacteria and viruses can both be destroyed using the same drugs.
_____

6. _____ True _____ False   Some of the most harmful superbugs seem to have developed in health care settings.
_____

7. _____ True _____ False   Labs can identify the right drug for a particular infection very quickly.
_____

8. _____ True _____ False   There is nothing people can do to prevent bacterial infections.
_____

Reading Analysis

Read each question carefully. Circle the number or letter of the correct answer, or write your answer in the space provided.

1. Review your answers to question #2 in the Prereading activity on page 112. Were all your answers correct? _____ Yes _____ No

2. Read lines 1–5.
    a. What are **antibiotics**?

    _____

    b. **Destroy** means
        1. stop.
        2. locate.
        3. kill.
    c. **Losing their punch** means
        1. losing their ability to kill bacteria.
        2. losing their ability to find bacteria.
        3. losing their ability to weaken bacteria.
    d. **Certain bacteria are now unbeatable with today's medicines.** This sentence means that
        1. today's medicines can stop certain bacteria.
        2. today's medicines are ineffective against some bacteria.
        3. today's medicines can beat all bacteria.
    e. **Drug-resistant** bacteria are
        1. bacteria that are very difficult to kill with many drugs.
        2. bacteria that can never be killed with many drugs.
        3. bacteria that are always killed with antibiotics.

3. Read lines 6–8.
    a. **Strains** means
        1. types.
        2. amounts.
        3. effects.
    b. **Infect** means
        1. resist.
        2. kill.
        3. make sick.

4. Read lines 9–12.

a. **Prescribe** means

   1. give someone a common antibiotic.
   2. give someone instructions to take certain medicine.
   3. advise someone how to treat an illness.

b. What are **viruses**?

_____

c. Where did you find this information?

_____

d. This type of information is called a(n) _____.

e. Which of the following illnesses can be caused by bacteria? Which are caused by viruses? Write *B* for bacteria and *V* for viruses on the line next to each illness.

   _____ 1. Eye infections
   _____ 2. Colds
   _____ 3. Strep throat
   _____ 4. Flu
   _____ 5. Ear infections
   _____ 6. Pneumonia

5. Read lines 13–21.

a. **Unfortunately** means

   1. sadly.
   2. surprisingly.
   3. luckily.

b. **Overuse** of a drug means

   1. take too much of a drug too often.
   2. take a drug for the wrong illness.

c. **Misuse** means

   1. take too much of a drug too often.
   2. take a drug for the wrong illness.

d. We **overuse** a drug when we

   1. take twice the prescribed amount of the drug.
   2. take an antibiotic for a viral infection.

e. We **misuse** a drug when we

   1. take twice the prescribed amount of the drug.
   2. take an antibiotic for a viral infection.

f. **Survive** means

   1. become weaker.
   2. start to die.
   3. continue to live.

6. Read lines 22–26.

    a. **Thrive** means

        1. kill quickly.

        2. grow successfully.

        3. become bigger.

    b. **Traits** are

        1. dangers.

        2. infections.

        3. characteristics.

    c. **Emerging** means

        1. speeding up.

        2. strengthening.

        3. appearing.

7. Read lines 28–31.

    a. **Don't insist on an antibiotic if your health care provider advises otherwise.**

    This sentence means

        1. if you want an antibiotic and your health care provider does not agree with you, then say you want one anyway.

        2. if your health care provider does not want to prescribe an antibiotic for you, then don't say you want one anyway.

    b. **Insist** means

        1. take.

        2. demand.

        3. advise.

    c. **Delaying** means

        1. waiting.

        2. arguing.

        3. hurrying.

    d. **Recover** means

        1. get worse.

        2. get better.

        3. do not improve.

8. Read lines 35–37. **"Treating infections with antibiotics is something we want to preserve for generations to come, so we shouldn't misuse them,"** says Dr. Julie Segre.
Dr. Segre means

    a. we want to be able to use antibiotics in the future, so we need to be careful now to use them properly.

    b. we want generations to preserve antibiotics for treating infections.

9. Read lines 38–40.

   a. **Confined to** means
      1. restricted to.
      2. started in.
      3. become dangerous in.

   b. **People who are sick or in a weakened state are more susceptible to picking up infections** means these people are
      1. more likely to get an infection.
      2. probably won't get an infection.
      3. always get an infection.

   c. **Susceptible** means
      1. frightened.
      2. worried.
      3. vulnerable.

10. In line 43, **MRSA** is
   a. an infection.
   b. an antibiotic.
   c. a superbug.

11. Read lines 46–53.

   a. **Potent** means
      1. common.
      2. powerful.
      3. dangerous.

   b. **Ideally** means
      1. as a good idea.
      2. in a quick way.
      3. in a perfect way.

   c. **Stubborn** means
      1. strong.
      2. dangerous.
      3. persistent.

12. What is the main idea of the passage?
   a. Some bacteria are becoming very resistant and cannot be killed, so we need to try to prevent infections and use antibiotics only when necessary.
   b. Bacteria cause serious infections that are treated with modern antibiotics, but sometimes people overuse or misuse them.
   c. People contribute to the spread of bacterial infections by not washing their hands, sharing personal items, and using antibiotics for viral infections.

Vocabulary Skills

Recognizing Word Forms

In English, some verbs change to nouns by adding *-tion* or *-ion*, for example, *react (v.)*, *reaction (n.)*.

Complete each sentence with the correct word form on the left. Use the correct form of the verb in either the affirmative or negative. The nouns may be singular or plural.

create *(v.)*

creation *(n.)*

1. Over time, the overuse and misuse of antibiotics _____ superbugs. The _____ of this stubborn bacteria happened over a long period of time.

digest *(v.)*

digestion *(n.)*

2. Some bacteria help you _____ your food. These "good" bacteria are a very important part of your _____.

infect *(v.)*

infection *(n.)*

3. Many hospital patients get a variety of dangerous _____ because their immune systems are weak. Superbugs _____ sick people quickly.

prescribe *(v.)*

prescription *(n.)*

4. Doctors often _____ antibiotics for some types of pneumonia. These _____ can only be written by a health care provider.

prevent *(v.)*

prevention *(n.)*

5. The _____ of bacterial infections is very important. It's essential to wash our hands frequently with soap and water. Water alone _____ illnesses from spreading.

Using Common Expressions and Idioms

Many common expressions and idioms are very useful. Knowing them helps you understand text and enables you to express your own ideas more clearly.

Match each expression with the correct meaning.

1. _____ do our part
2. _____ in the first place
3. _____ keep ahead of
4. _____ lose their punch
5. _____ make an educated guess
6. _____ run out of

a. become weaker
b. predict after careful thought
c. take responsibility
d. deplete or use something up
e. to begin with
f. maintain an advantage

Use the correct expressions in the exercise below: *do our part, in the first place, keep ahead of, lose their punch, make an educated guess,* or *run out of*. Use each expression only once.

1. Some doctors believe that one day we may _____ effective antibiotics. Then we will be unable to treat many diseases.

2. Researchers are studying which diseases require antibiotics _____. It's not helpful to take antibiotics for an illness that an antibiotic cannot cure.

3. Doctors must sometimes _____ whether or not an infection requires antibiotics because it often takes days to get lab results.

4. We must _____ to stop the spread of infections by not sharing personal items with other people.

5. Some antibiotics _____ after just a few months. As a result, they can become ineffective quickly.

6. Scientists are trying to _____ drug-resistant superbugs by developing new drugs first.

Vocabulary in Context

Read the following sentences. Complete each sentence with the correct word from the box. Use each word only once.

confined *(v.)*	ideally *(adv.)*	recovered *(v.)*	susceptible *(adj.)*
delayed *(v.)*	misuse *(n.)*	stubborn *(adj.)*	thrive *(v.)*
destroyed *(v.)*	potent *(adj.)*		

1. The earthquake in Los Angeles _____ many buildings and homes around the city.

2. Because of the students' _____ of cell phones, the teacher no longer allows them in class.

3. The sick kitten began to _____ after Lena fed her and kept her warm.

4. The bus was _____ because of the heavy snowstorm. As a result, I was late for school.

5. Jack _____ from his cold after only a few days. Then he was able to return to work.

6. We _____ our new puppy to the kitchen so that he wouldn't chew on the living room furniture.

7. People who work in hospitals are usually more _____ to getting sick.

8. This medicine is very _____. You cannot take more than one pill a day.

9. _____, students should do their homework immediately after class. However, most students wait until much later to complete their assignments.

10. The _____ little boy refused to put on his coat even though it was a very cold day.

Reading Skill

Understanding Graphics

Graphics, including chains of events and line graphs, may accompany a reading. They often illustrate information in the reading. Understanding this type of illustration increases your understanding of a reading.

Look at the graphic below. Match each statement to a letter on the graphic. Then write the correct letter next to each statement.

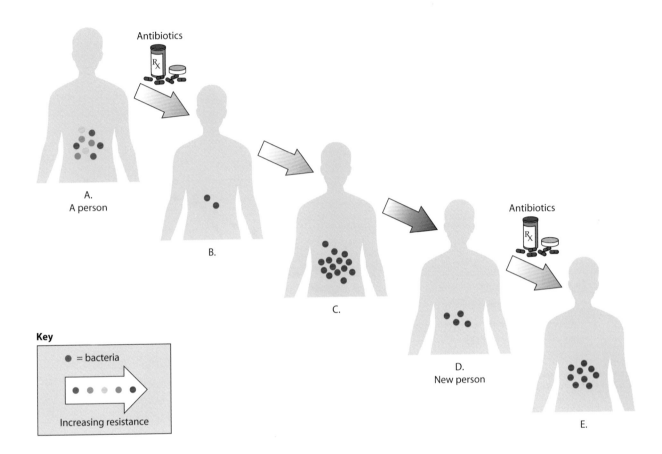

A.
A person

B.

C.

D.
New person

E.

Antibiotics

Antibiotics

Key

● = bacteria

Increasing resistance

_____ Antibiotics fail to kill resistant bacteria.

_____ Resistant bacteria infect a new person.

_____ Resistant and non-resistant bacteria population infects a person.

_____ Antibiotics kill non-resistant bacteria.

_____ Resistant bacteria multiply.

Review the line graph below. Then answer the questions that follow.

Increasing incidence of antibiotic-resistant infections

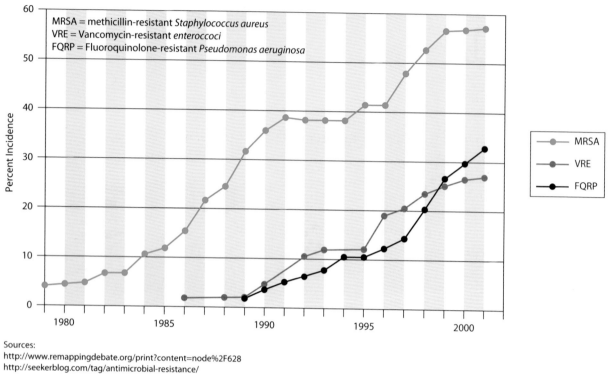

MRSA = methicillin-resistant *Staphylococcus aureus*
VRE = Vancomycin-resistant *enteroccoci*
FQRP = Fluoroquinolone-resistant *Pseudomonas aeruginosa*

Sources:
http://www.remappingdebate.org/print?content=node%2F628
http://seekerblog.com/tag/antimicrobial-resistance/

1. When did methicillin-resistant *Staphylococcus aureus* (MRSA) bacteria begin to become resistant to antibiotics?
   a. 1979
   b. 1982
   c. 1983

2. How long did it take for MRSA to become drug resistant at least 58 percent of the time?
   a. 17 years
   b. 24 years
   c. 34 years

3. When did Vancomycin-resistant *enteroccoci* (VRE) first become resistant to antibiotics?
   a. About 1987
   b. About 1989
   c. About 1990

4. How long did it take for VRE to become drug resistant at least 25 percent of the time?
   a. 10 years
   b. 12 years
   c. 16 years

5. When did Fluoroquinolone-resistant *Pseudomonas aeruginosa* (FQRP) first become resistant to antibiotics?
   a. By 1990
   b. By 1991
   c. By 1992

6. How long did it take for FQRP to become drug resistant at least 30 percent of the time?
   a. 7 years
   b. 10 years
   c. 12 years

7. What conclusion can we draw from these statistics?
   a. It is impossible to create a drug that will always kill all bacteria.
   b. Bacteria are becoming resistant to new drugs at a faster rate.
   c. Bacteria are stronger than any drug that researchers can develop.

Information Recall

Review the information in the chain of events and line graph above. Then answer the questions.

1. What does "resistant bacteria" mean?

   _____

   _____

   _____

2. How do resistant bacteria multiply?

   _____

   _____

   _____

3. Which antibiotic-resistant infection has increased the most since the 1980s?

_____

_____

_____

4. What do you think will happen in the future? Do you think superbugs are unbeatable? Why or why not?

_____

_____

_____

Writing a Summary

A summary is a short paragraph that provides the most important information in a reading. It usually does not include details, just main ideas. When you write a summary, it is important to use your own words and not copy directly from the reading.

Write a brief summary of the passage. It should not be more than five sentences. Use your own words. Be sure to indent the first line.

_____

_____

_____

_____

_____

_____

_____

Topics for Discussion and Writing

1. What are ways to prevent bacterial infections and to use antibiotics properly? Check (√) all that apply.
   _____ a. Wash your hands frequently with hand sanitizers.
   _____ b. Take the exact amount of antibiotics your health care provider prescribes.
   _____ c. Try to prevent the spread of bacteria by not sharing personal items.
   _____ d. Take antibiotics for viral infections.
   _____ e. Wash your hands frequently with soap and water.
   _____ f. Ask for an antibiotic as soon as you have an infection.
   _____ g. Take extra antibiotics so you can recover more quickly.
   _____ h. Take antibiotics only if they are prescribed for you.
   _____ i. Share personal items as long as they are clean.

2. Are antibiotics very commonly used in your culture? Why or why not? Discuss your answers with your classmates.

3. This article states that the best way to prevent bacterial infections is by washing your hands with soap and water. What are some other things that we can do to prevent the spread of bacterial infections? Work with a partner and make a list. Then compare your list with your classmates' lists.

4. Write in your journal. Why do you think many people overuse and misuse antibiotics? Explain your answer.

Critical Thinking

1. According to this article, many parents expect doctors to prescribe antibiotics for a child's ear infection even though an antibiotic may not be necessary. Why do you think many parents do this? Discuss this with a partner.

2. In the past, superbugs have been confined to health care settings. Now, however, these infections are out in the community. What do you think is the reason for this? Give examples and share your ideas with your classmates.

3. Dr. Julie Segre of the NIH says, "Treating infections with antibiotics is something we want to preserve for generations to come, so we shouldn't misuse them." What do you think Dr. Segre believes about most people's use of antibiotics? What do you think she fears about the future of antibiotics?

Crossword Puzzle

Review the words in the box below. Then read the clues on the next page. Write the words in the correct spaces in the puzzle.

antibiotics	insist	recover	thrive
confined	misuse	resistant	traits
delaying	overuse	strains	unbeatable
destroy	potent	survive	unfortunately
ideally	prescribe	susceptible	viruses
infection			

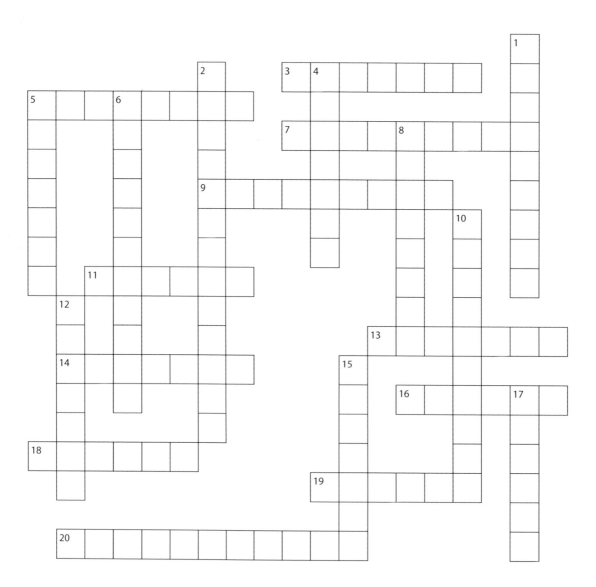

Crossword Puzzle Clues

ACROSS CLUES

3. The doctor prescribed two pills a day, but you took four pills today. Don't _____ the drugs!

5. Sometimes _____, or putting off, taking a drug is the best course of action. The drug may not be necessary after all.

7. Doctors need to be careful when they _____ drugs. Sometimes the drugs are not necessary.

9. Many types of bacteria are now _____ to even the most powerful drugs we have today.

11. Many drugs are powerful, but even the most _____ ones are not working well any more.

13. _____, doctors could get lab results quickly to help them identify the appropriate drug.

14. Sometimes, people can _____ from an infection without the use of drugs.

16. Some bacteria can share their _____, or characteristics, with other bacteria.

18. Do not _____ on getting medicine to kill bacteria if your doctor believes you do not need it.

19. Whenever you take an antibacterial drug when it's unnecessary, you _____ the drug.

20. People who are weak or already sick are very _____ to infections. They get infections very easily.

DOWN CLUES

1. You can get a(n) _____ if you have a cut and do not keep it clean.

2. _____, it is becoming increasingly difficult to develop drugs that can kill bacteria.

4. _____ are microorganisms that cannot grow or reproduce on their own.

5. It is becoming more and more difficult to _____ harmful bacteria with the drugs we have today.

6. _____ are drugs that fight bacteria.

8. Some harmful bacteria are not _____ to hospitals. They have spread to the general public.

10. Some bacteria appear to be _____. Nothing seems to kill them.

12. Some of the _____ of bacteria that developed in hospitals have spread outside.

15. Drugs cannot kill all bacteria. New drugs must be developed to kill the bacteria that _____.

17. Many bacteria that are not killed continue to _____ and spread.

CHAPTER 8

It's Time for a Conversation: Learning the Language of Dolphins

Prereading

1. What kinds of animals communicate with each other? How do they communicate?

2. Do you think animals can communicate with people? Why or why not?

3. Read the title of the chapter and look at the photo. Who do you think these women are? What do you think they are doing?

4. What do you know about dolphins? For example, how long do they live? Where do they live? How do they communicate with each other? Write your information in the box below.

Information about Dolphins

Reading

🎧 **Read the passage carefully. Then complete the exercises that follow.**

CD 2
TR 3

It's Time for a Conversation: Learning the Language of Dolphins

by Joshua Foer, *National Geographic*

Head trainer Teri Turner Bolton looks out at two young adult male dolphins, Hector and Han, whose beaks, or rostra, are poking above the water as they eagerly await a command. The bottlenose dolphins at the Roatán Institute for Marine Sciences (RIMS), a resort and research institution on an island off the coast of Honduras, are
5 old pros at dolphin performance art. They've been trained to corkscrew, or spin through the air on command, skate backward across the surface of the water while standing upright on their tails, and wave their pectoral fins at the tourists who arrive several times a week on cruise ships.

But the scientists at RIMS are more interested in how the dolphins think than in
10 what they can do. When given the hand signal to "innovate," Hector and Han know to dip below the surface and blow a bubble, or arch out of the water, or dive down to the ocean floor, or perform any of the dozen or so other movements, but not to repeat anything they've already done during that session. Incredibly, they usually understand that they're supposed to keep trying some new behavior each session.

15 Bolton presses her palms together over her head, the signal to innovate, and then puts her fists together, the sign for "tandem." With those two gestures, she has

instructed the dolphins to show her a behavior she hasn't seen during this session and to do it in unison, or at the same time.

20 Hector and Han disappear beneath the surface. With them is a psychologist named Stan Kuczaj, wearing a wet suit and snorkel gear and carrying a large underwater video camera with hydrophones. He records several seconds of audible chirping between Hector and Han, then his camera captures them both slowly rolling over in unison and flapping their tails three times simultaneously.

There are two possible explanations of this remarkable behavior. Either one dolphin 25 is mimicking the other so quickly and precisely that the apparent coordination is only an illusion. Or it's not an illusion at all: When they whistle back and forth beneath the surface, they're literally discussing a plan.

Dolphins are extraordinarily garrulous. Not only do they whistle and click, but they also make loud sounds to discipline their young and chase away sharks. Scientists 30 listening to all these sounds have long wondered what, if anything, they might mean. Surely such a large-brained, highly social creature wouldn't waste all that energy babbling beneath the waves unless the vocalizations contained some sort of meaningful content. And yet despite a half century of study, nobody can say what the fundamental units of dolphin vocalization are. "If we can find a pattern connecting 35 vocalization to behavior, it'll be a huge deal," says Kuczaj, 64, who has published more scientific articles on dolphin cognition than almost anyone else in the field. He believes that his work with the synchronized dolphins at RIMS may prove to be a key that unlocks dolphin communication, though he adds, "The sophistication of dolphins that makes them so interesting also makes them really difficult to study."

40 Dolphins use distinct "signature whistles" to identify and call to one another. Each dolphin is thought to invent a unique name for itself as a calf and to keep it for life. Dolphins greet one another at sea by exchanging signature whistles and seem to remember the signature whistles of other dolphins for decades. Though other species make sounds that refer to predators, no other animal besides humans is believed to 45 have specific labels for individuals.

Denise Herzing has spent the past three decades getting to know more than 300 individual Atlantic spotted dolphins spanning three generations. She works a 175-square-mile of ocean off the Bahamas, in the longest-running underwater wild-dolphin program in the world. Because of its crystal clear waters, it's a place where 50 dolphin researchers can spend extended periods observing and interacting with wild animals.

When Herzing was 12 years old, she entered a scholarship contest that required her to answer the question "What would you do for the world if you could do one thing?" Her reply: "I would develop a human-animal translator so that we can 55 understand other minds on the planet."

Now, in her underwater sessions, face-to-face with dolphins, Herzing has recorded and logged thousands of hours of footage of every kind of dolphin behavior using a

CHAT box.[1] Herzing has known most of her dolphins since birth, and she knows their mothers, aunts, and grandmothers as well. Their life span can be more than 50 years.

60   When the opportunity finally arrives to test the CHAT box in the wild, the two dolphins that swim up to her boat are ones that Herzing has been hoping to encounter all week: Meridian and Nereide. Indeed, recordings of both dolphins' signature whistles have been preprogrammed into the CHAT boxes in the hope that Herzing might get a chance to greet the dolphins and interact with them. These two females

65   represent the best candidates for Herzing's work. They haven't yet become pregnant and are still just kids, with lots of curiosity and lots of freedom to play and explore.

    After an hour, the dolphins began to lose interest. As Nereide turned to leave, she made one final long, mysterious whistle, looked back at us, and then swam off into the blue darkness and disappeared.

---

[1] A **CHAT box** is a computer that can broadcast prerecorded dolphins' signature whistles as well as dolphin-like whistles into the ocean and record any sounds that dolphins whistle back.

Fact Finding

Read the passage again. Then read the following statements. Check (√) whether each statement is True or False. If a statement is false, rewrite it so that it is true. Then go back to the passage and find the line that supports your answer.

1. _____ True _____ False   The dolphins at RIMS are trained to perform on command.

_____

2. _____ True _____ False   The tourists who watch the dolphins are interested in how the dolphins think.

_____

3. _____ True _____ False   Teri Turner Bolton is a scientist.

_____

4. _____ True _____ False   Stan Kuczaj studies the dolphins by recording their sounds and movements.

_____

5. _____ True _____ False   Dolphins are easy to study because they are very intelligent.

_____

6. _____ True _____ False   Dolphins may have specific whistles to identify other dolphins.

_____

7. _____ True _____ False   A CHAT box records video of dolphins.

_____

Reading Analysis

Read each question carefully. Circle the letter or number of the correct answer, or write your answer in the space provided.

1. Read lines 1–3.
   a. **Rostra** means
      1. tails.
      2. dolphins.
      3. beaks.
   b. **Whose** refers to
      1. the trainer.
      2. the dolphins.
      3. the people.

2. Read lines 3–8.
   a. **Old pros** means that the dolphins
      1. have a lot of experience.
      2. are very intelligent.
      3. live in Honduras.
   b. Which of these are examples of **dolphin performance art**?
      1. Skating backward on command
      2. Waving their fins at the tourists
      3. Both 1 and 2

3. In line 10, **innovate** means
   a. do something in a new way.
   b. communicate something in a new way.
   c. understand something in a new way.

4. Read lines 15–18.
   a. What is Bolton's signal to the dolphins to innovate?
      1. She puts her fists together.
      2. She blows a whistle.
      3. She presses her palms together.
   b. **Tandem** refers to
      1. working as a team.
      2. showing a new behavior.
      3. giving a signal or sign.

c. **In unison** means
   1. as a pair.
   2. at the same time.
   3. quickly.

5. Read lines 19–23.
a. **Hydrophones** record
   1. video under water.
   2. sounds under water.
   3. movements under water.
b. Something **audible** is something you can
   1. see.
   2. hear.
   3. touch.
c. **Simultaneously** means
   1. very hard.
   2. very slowly.
   3. in unison.

6. Read lines 24–26.
a. What is this **remarkable behavior**?
   1. Hector and Han chirp to each other and then move in unison.
   2. Hector and Han copy each other's movements.
   3. The video camera and hydrophones record sound and movement.
b. **Remarkable** means
   1. careful.
   2. impressive.
   3. practiced.
c. **Mimicking** means
   1. trying.
   2. recording.
   3. copying.
d. **Precisely** means
   1. intelligently.
   2. exactly.
   3. noisily.
e. **Apparent** means
   1. planned.
   2. obvious.
   3. correct.

f. An **illusion** is
1. a proven fact.
2. a false impression.
3. a recorded observation.

7. Read lines 28–29.
a. **Garrulous** means
1. friendly.
2. talkative.
3. intelligent.
b. What are two reasons dolphins make loud sounds?
Give two examples.

1. _____

2. _____

8. Read lines 31–38.
a. **Vocalization** refers to
1. making sounds to communicate.
2. making meaningless sounds.
3. making sounds under water.
b. **Cognition** refers to
1. behavior and training.
2. noise or communication.
3. thought or understanding.
c. **Synchronized** means
1. set to occur at the same time.
2. highly intelligent and cooperative.
3. very well trained to behave.

9. Read line 40.
a. **Distinct** means
1. social.
2. loud and clear.
3. recognizable.
b. Dolphins use **signature whistles** to
1. communicate with their trainers.
2. greet and identify other dolphins.
3. learn new behavior.

10. Read lines 46–55. Which of the following sentences about Denise Herzing are true? Check (√) all that are correct.

_____ a. She is a dolphin trainer.

_____ b. She researches dolphin behavior.

_____ c. She has wanted to study animal communication since she was a child.

_____ d. She studies dolphins off the coast of Honduras.

_____ e. She is familiar with several generations of related dolphins.

_____ f. She is able to translate the dolphins' vocalizations into English.

11. Read lines 56–58.

a. **Logged** means that you

1. observed something carefully.
2. wrote down something you observed.
3. came face-to-face with animals or people.

b. What is a CHAT box?

_____

c. Where did you find this information?

_____

d. This type of information is called

1. a preface.
2. an index.
3. a footnote.

12. Read lines 60–62. **Encounter** means

a. meet.
b. record.
c. observe.

13. Read lines 62–64. **Interact with** means

a. play with.
b. communicate with.
c. make recordings of.

14. Read line 67. **After an hour, the dolphins began to lose interest** means

a. the dolphins started to go away.
b. the dolphins started to get tired.
c. the dolphins started to get bored.

15. What is the main idea of the passage?

a. Dolphin behavior is very interesting to watch and study.
b. Scientists are trying to understand dolphin communication.
c. Dolphins communicate with each other through vocalization.

Vocabulary Skills

PART 1

Recognizing Word Forms

In English, some adjectives become adverbs by adding the suffix *-ly,* for example, *slow (adj.),* *slowly (adv.).*

Complete each sentence with the correct word form on the left.

garrulous *(adj.)*

garrulously *(adv.)*

1. Dolphins whistle, click, and make loud sounds. They are very _____ animals. They also _____ greet each other.

incredible *(adj.)*

incredibly *(adv.)*

2. Dolphins are _____ intelligent. Scientists study their _____ vocalization and communication skills.

precise *(adj.)*

precisely *(adv.)*

3. The trainers observe the _____ movements of the dolphins. They are amazed at how the dolphins copy each other so _____ .

remarkable *(adj.)*

remarkably *(adv.)*

4. Scientists believe it is _____ that the dolphins understand the trainers' hand signals. _____ , the dolphins seem to understand the request for new behaviors, too.

simultaneous *(adj.)*

simultaneously *(adv.)*

5. Hector and Han _____ perform in unison. It's difficult for the scientists to understand and explain the dolphins' _____ behavior.

PART 2

Synonyms

Synonyms are words with similar meanings. For example, *anxious* and *worried* are synonyms.

Read each sentence. Write the synonym of the word or phrase in parentheses in the space provided. Use each word or phrase only once.

apparent	encounter	in unison	mimic
distinct	garrulous	logged	precisely

1. Like many people, dolphins are very _____ (*talkative*). They appear to enjoy communicating with each other.

2. Young children often _____ (*copy*) the behavior of older children and adults before they understand what they are doing.

3. The group of performers danced across the stage and then all leaped into the air

   _____ (*simultaneously*).

4. The _____ (*obvious*) ability of dolphins to communicate ideas and make decisions requires further research.

5. No one wants to _____ (*meet by chance*) a shark while swimming in the ocean.

6. John's way of talking is very _____ (*recognizable*). When he calls me on the phone, I know his voice immediately.

7. Our class begins at _____ (*exactly*) 9:00 a.m. The professor does not allow students who are late to enter the class.

8. The researcher carefully _____ (*noted*) the day and time of each dolphin observation she made, as well as each animal's actions.

Vocabulary in Context

Read the following sentences. Complete each sentence with the correct word or phrase from the box. Use each word or phrase only once.

audible *(adj.)*	hydrophones *(n.)*	in tandem	interact *(v.)*
cognition *(n.)*	illusion *(n.)*	innovated *(v.)*	synchronized *(v.)*

1. When the magician made the coins disappear, it was only a(n) _____. In reality, the coins were in his sleeve.

2. Kate and I carefully _____ the time on our watches so that we would arrive at the theater at the same time.

3. The Olympic ice skaters performed _____. Each jump and spin was done together at the precise moment.

4. A baby's _____ increases as she grows up and learns about her environment.

5. It's important for young children to _____ with other children their own age so they can learn to socialize.

6. Scuba divers often use _____ to detect when a boat or ship is nearby.

7. Please raise the volume on the music. It's barely _____, and I'd like to hear it.

8. When Daniel's company began to fail, he _____ a new business plan to help his company become successful again.

Reading Skill

Creating an Outline

Creating an outline is a very useful skill. It can help you understand and remember the most important information from a reading.

Read the article again. Underline what you think are the main ideas. Then scan the article and complete the following outline, using the sentences that you have underlined to help you. You will use this outline later to answer specific questions about the article.

I. Introduction

    A. _____

    B. The dolphins have been trained to perform many actions.

        1. corkscrew, or spin, through the air on command, etc.

II. Scientists want to know how dolphins think.

    A. Scientists give Hector and Han a hand signal to "innovate."

        1. _____

    B. Bolton gives the signal "tandem."

        1. _____

III. There are two possible explanations for the dolphins' behavior.

    A. _____

    B. _____

IV. Dolphins have an interesting nature and behavior.

    A. _____

    B. _____

V. Scientists think some dolphin behavior might be meaningful.

    A. Dolphins use distinct "signature whistles" to identify and call to one another.

    B. _____

    C. _____

    D. _____

VI. Denise Herzing has done extensive research with dolphins.

    A. _____

    B. _____

Information Recall

Review each question carefully. Use the outline to answer the questions. Do not refer back to the text.

    1. What do scientists want to know about dolphins?

        _____

        _____

    2. What are two possible explanations for the dolphins' unusual behavior?

        a. _____

        b. _____

    3. Why do scientists think that the dolphin's remarkable behavior is meaningful, and not just learned through training?

        _____

        _____

    4. How does Denise Herzing study the dolphins?

        _____

        _____

Writing a Summary

A summary is a short paragraph that provides the most important information in a reading. It usually does not include details, just main ideas. When you write a summary, it is important to use your own words and not copy directly from the reading.

Write a brief summary of the passage. It should not be more than five sentences. Use your own words. Be sure to indent the first line.

_____

_____

_____

_____

_____

_____

Topics for Discussion and Writing

1. Do you think it's useful for scientists to study communication between animals such as dolphins? Why or why not? Work with a partner. Give reasons and examples to support your opinion.

2. Dr. Herzing has known most of her dolphins since birth, and she knows their mothers, aunts, and grandmothers as well. Why do you think Dr. Herzing apparently only studies female dolphins? What does the fact that the dolphins appear to be related imply about dolphin social groups? Think about these two questions, and discuss your ideas with your classmates.

3. Write in your journal. Dr. Denise Herzing has wanted to understand animals since she was a child. When you were a child, what did you want to do when you grew up? Did your ideas change as you got older?

Critical Thinking

1. In the passage, psychologist Stan Kuczaj says, "The sophistication of dolphins that makes them so interesting also makes them really difficult to study." (p. 132, lines 38–39). What is Kuczaj's opinion of dolphins? Why does he think they are difficult to study? Think about these questions, then discuss your ideas with your classmates.

2. Researchers are trying to develop ways to communicate with dolphins. If they are eventually able to converse with dolphins, what would be the advantages to doing so? What might be the disadvantages to doing so?

3. Dolphins are often used by the military. They are trained to do dangerous work such as mine (an explosive device) detection and clearance. Do you agree with using intelligent animals for this purpose? Why or why not?

4. What do you think is the tone of this article? Do you think that the people quoted in the reading are optimistic that we will be able to understand dolphin communication one day? Explain your reasons for your opinion.

Crossword Puzzle

Review the words in the box below. Then read the clues on the next page. Write the words in the correct spaces in the puzzle.

apparent
audible
cognition
distinct
encounter

garrulous
hydrophone
illusion
innovate
interact

logged
mimicking
performance
precisely
remarkable

simultaneously
synchronized
tandem
vocalizations

Crossword Puzzle Clues

ACROSS CLUES

2. A(n) _____ is a device for hearing and recording sounds under water.

4. Clearly, dolphins are _____ animals. They are amazing!

6. Herzing has _____ thousands of hours of notes and recordings over the years, yet she still has more research to do.

8. For some people, animal intelligence is just a(n) _____. For others, animal intelligence is very real.

10. Researchers want to study the dolphins' _____ ability to communicate with each other.

14. Dolphins like to _____ with people. They are especially eager to play with people.

17. The two dolphins rose out of the water and flew through a hoop in _____.

18. The two animals _____ their movements so that their timing was perfect.

19. Dolphins are not the only animals that can _____. Some primates, such as chimpanzees, can create simple tools to solve a problem like obtaining food.

DOWN CLUES

1. Dolphin _____ are incomprehensible to us, but they have meaning for each other.

3. Some sounds that dolphins make are not _____ to humans. We cannot hear them.

5. As part of their act, the two dolphins rose into the air, twisted, and dove back into the water _____. How can they move together at the same time?

7. The level of _____ in dolphins appears to be very high. They seem to be able to think.

9. Dolphins make very _____ sounds that other dolphins understand.

11. People of all ages enjoy watching a(n) _____ of dolphins at an aquarium. The acts are very entertaining.

12. The dolphins coordinate their movements so _____ that they seem to act as a single unit.

13. When dolphins _____ a shark, they make sounds to chase the shark away.

15. Dolphins are very _____. Researchers wonder what they are "saying" to each other.

16. A dolphin's act of _____ another dolphin may not be copying at all. It may really be a way of communicating ideas.

Prereading

1. Today, we enjoy considerable technology everywhere in our lives. Where do you think some of this technology came from? Who developed it?

2. Do you think governments should spend more money or less money studying outer space? Why?

3. Read the title of this article and look at the two photos. What is the connection between them?

Reading

🎧 **Read the passage carefully. Then complete the exercises that follow.**

CD 2
TR 4

Space Science on Earth
National Space and Aeronautics Administration (NASA)

Outer space has always fascinated people. They are curious about the planets and our solar system. They want to know what stars are made of, and how far away they are. They are curious about the nature of the universe. Scientists have been studying astronomy for centuries, but only from Earth—until they developed technology
5   to send spacecraft into space to look deeper and farther than anyone could have imagined even 100 years ago.

Studying space is very expensive, and can only be done on a large scale, with considerable funding. In 1958, The National Aeronautics and Space Administration (NASA) was created. It is the U.S. government agency that is responsible for the
10   U.S. space program and aerospace research. One of NASA's many purposes is to encourage peaceful applications, or uses, of space science.

Although most people understand the importance of space science, they sometimes wonder why billions of dollars are spent on space missions and research. How does this research and technology help people on Earth? In fact, it does—through spinoff
15   technology.

What Is a Spinoff?

A NASA spinoff is a technology that was originally developed for the space program and now provides benefits for the nation and the world as a commercial product or service. NASA spinoffs enhance many aspects of daily life, including health and medicine, transportation, public safety, consumer goods, energy, the
20   environment, and information technology. Here are just a few of the hundreds of examples of spinoff technology in our communities and our homes.

Spinoff Technology in Our Homes and Communities

Spinoff technology can help to make our homes and communities safer and more comfortable places to live. Most people are aware that carbon monoxide (CO) buildup in our homes can be very dangerous. This may come from a faulty furnace
25   or fireplace. As a result, some people have carbon monoxide detectors in their homes, but these detectors only alert them if the level of carbon monoxide is unsafe. However, using space technology, NASA developed an air-conditioning system that can not only detect dangerous amounts of carbon monoxide, but actually oxidizes the

toxic gases into harmless carbon dioxide (CO_2). This kind of development makes us realize that removing safety hazards is far better than creating alarms to detect them.

In addition to helping people to have clean air, having access to clean water is also of major importance for everyone. NASA engineers have been working with private companies to create better systems for clean, drinkable water for astronauts in space. These systems, which have been developed for the astronauts, can quickly and affordably cleanse any available water. This is a major advantage to the people on Earth who live in remote or developing areas where water is scarce or polluted.

Yet another area of concern to people everywhere is the safety and quality of the food they eat. In order to improve food quality for astronauts on lengthy space missions, NASA conducted extensive research and worked with several food companies to find solutions. One result was the freeze-drying process. This process allows food to be kept for long periods without refrigeration, while still retaining 98 percent of its nutritional value but only 20 percent of its original weight. Freeze-dried food can be very useful to many people, especially those who live where electricity is not always dependable.

Space technology has also helped to improve what we wear. Ordinary clothing tends to trap heat and sweat during intense activity in cold weather. Using the same technology that is applied to space suits, NASA worked with the clothing industry to create new "phase change" materials. These new materials moderate, or control, temperatures between the body and the environment, making our clothing more comfortable, especially during physical activities such as running or biking.

Spinoff Technology in Medicine

Spinoff technology has been applied effectively in many other areas too, including the field of medicine. Astronomy technology that was once used to measure the temperature of distant stars and planets now measures the temperature of humans. A hand-held, high-speed medical thermometer can measure a person's temperature in less than two seconds. Since it doesn't touch the body, it eliminates the risk of infection. This makes it faster—and safer—for people to use.

Advanced extended-wear contact lenses were invented through research that could only be conducted in the weightlessness of outer space. Discoveries by NASA and private scientists led to the creation of lenses that are superior to previous "soft" contacts. The new versions are less susceptible to bacteria. As a result, there is a smaller chance that the new contact lenses will cause an infection. They are also easier to handle and hold their shape over time, so they provide sharper vision.

Another company that was working with NASA invented a new type of translucent, ceramic braces to help straighten teeth. These braces were created to meet the need for corrective dental wear. They are very effective and durable. Because the braces are translucent, it doesn't appear that the person is wearing them at all. The braces are one of the most successful orthodontic products ever introduced.

Spinoff Technology in Sports

Many people might be surprised to learn that spinoff technology is also extensively used in sports equipment. For example, because of the work of a NASA engineer who designed space suits, athletic shoes today reduce fatigue. The material that was used in space suits, which is extremely lightweight, is now used in athletic shoes. Not only are these shoes much lighter, they are stronger and longer-lasting than ever before.

Another example of spinoff technology is a new heart-monitoring device. This technology was created to keep track of the health of astronauts. It was modified, or adapted, by a company for use in physical fitness equipment. People can now wear this heartbeat monitor under their clothing to make them aware of their heart rate. This can help users monitor the intensity of their exercise. Some people who may benefit from using this device include patients with cardiac illnesses who need to be careful when they exercise, as well as top athletes who are training to reach their ultimate physical condition.

The products and research that have come out of the space programs are numerous and useful to us in our everyday lives. New spinoff technology is constantly being developed, then transferred to industry and to the public. We are all benefiting from the space program—through spinoff technology.

Fact Finding

Read the passage again. Then read the following statements. Check (√) whether each statement is True or False. If a statement is false, rewrite it so that it is true. Then go back to the passage and find the line that supports your answer.

1. _____ True _____ False   Scientists sent spacecraft into space as early as 100 years ago.

   _____

2. _____ True _____ False   Billions of dollars are spent on space missions and space research.

   _____

3. _____ True _____ False   NASA is an international space agency.

   _____

4. _____ True _____ False   NASA's air-conditioning system can change some dangerous gases into harmless ones.

   _____

5. _____ True _____ False   Properly freeze-dried food is just as nutritious as fresh food.

   _____

6. _____ True _____ False   A hand-held, high-speed medical thermometer has the same technology that was once used to measure the temperature of distant stars.

   _____

7. _____ True _____ False   Contact lenses have been improved through space research.

   _____

8. _____ True _____ False   People are benefiting from spinoff technology, but businesses are not.

   _____

Reading Analysis

Read each question carefully. Circle the letter or number of the correct answer, or write your answer in the space provided.

1. Read lines 3–6.
- a. **Nature** means
  1. trees and plants.
  2. qualities.
  3. location.
- b. **Universe** means
  1. stars.
  2. spacecraft.
  3. outer space.
- c. **Astronomy** is the science of
  1. space.
  2. technology.
  3. Earth.
- d. **Centuries** means
  1. thousands of years.
  2. hundreds of years.
  3. many decades.

2. Read lines 7–8.
- a. **A large scale** means
  1. a long time.
  2. a far distance.
  3. a great amount.
- b. **Considerable funding** means
  1. a lot of money.
  2. a great deal of thought.
  3. a lot of time.

3. In line 11, **applications** means
- a. uses.
- b. requests.
- c. research.

4. Read lines 16–18. A **spinoff** is space technology
- a. used only by astronauts on long space missions.
- b. developed for astronauts and now used by people everywhere.
- c. developed by NASA that is expensive.

5. Read lines 23–26.
  a. **Buildup** means
    1. construction.
    2. accumulation.
    3. problems.
  b. **Carbon monoxide (CO) buildup** in our homes is
    1. not safe.
    2. safe.
    3. common.
  c. What are two causes of **carbon monoxide buildup**?

    1. _____

    2. _____

  d. A **carbon monoxide detector**
    1. finds unsafe levels of carbon monoxide.
    2. changes unsafe levels of carbon monoxide.
    3. decreases unsafe levels of carbon monoxide.
  e. **Detect** means
    1. cause.
    2. locate.
    3. reduce.

6. Read lines 27–30.
  a. The **NASA air-conditioning system** can
    1. only detect dangerous amounts of carbon monoxide.
    2. change the dangerous gases into harmless ones.
    3. make a room feel cool in warm weather.
  b. **Toxic** and **harmless** are
    1. synonyms.
    2. antonyms.
  c. **Toxic** means
    1. deadly.
    2. gaseous.
    3. faulty.
  d. **Hazards** are
    1. gases.
    2. detectors.
    3. dangers.

7. Read lines 34–36.

    a. **Affordably** means

       1. rapidly.

       2. inexpensively.

       3. carefully.

    b. **Remote** means

       1. poor.

       2. dirty.

       3. distant.

    c. Water that is **scarce** is water that

       1. is available in very small amounts.

       2. needs to be purified.

       3. is only found as ice.

8. Read lines 38–40.

    a. **Lengthy** means

       1. short.

       2. long.

       3. far away.

    b. **Lengthy** and **extensive** are

       1. synonyms.

       2. antonyms.

9. In line 46, **intense** means

    a. powerful; strong.

    b. hot; sweaty.

    c. usual; common.

10. Read lines 48–49. What is a synonym for **moderate**?

_____

11. Read lines 55–56.

    a. It **eliminates the risk of infection** means it

       1. can help you recover from an illness faster.

       2. can prevent you from getting sick.

       3. can lower a person's temperature.

    b. **Eliminates** means

       1. gets rid of.

       2. helps.

       3. detects.

    c. What is an advantage of the high-speed medical thermometer?

_____

12. Read lines 58–62.

    a. **Superior to** means

        1. better than.

        2. larger than.

        3. cheaper than.

    b. In what ways are the new contact lenses **superior to** previous ones? Give two reasons:

        1. _____

        2. _____

13. Read lines 65–66.

    a. **Durable** means

        1. long-lasting.

        2. comfortable.

        3. useful.

    b. **Translucent** means

        1. thin.

        2. clear.

        3. strong.

14. Read lines 69–71.

    a. **Fatigue** means

        1. discomfort.

        2. energy.

        3. tiredness.

    b. Why does the new material now used in athletic shoes reduce fatigue?

    _____

15. What is the main idea of the passage?

    a. Spinoff technology from NASA space programs is extensive, and it has improved our lives in the home, outside the home, and in medicine.

    b. Spinoff technology was developed by NASA because many people criticized the high cost of space programs.

    c. There are many examples of spinoff technology, such as freeze-dried food, heartbeat monitors, and lightweight athletic shoes.

Vocabulary Skills

PART 1

Recognizing Word Forms

In English, some nouns become adjectives by adding the suffix -ful, for example, power (n.), powerful (adj.).

Complete each sentence with the correct word form on the left. All the nouns are singular.

harm *(n.)*

harmful *(adj.)*

  1. High levels of carbon monoxide in the home can cause _____ to people. _____ gases are changed to nonpoisonous ones with the use of these new systems.

help *(n.)*

helpful *(adj.)*

  2. Spinoff technology can be very _____ in rural areas where water is sparse or polluted. These new systems are a great _____ to people who do not have easy access to safe, drinkable water.

care *(n.)*

careful *(adj.)*

  3. Patients with cardiac illness should be _____ when they exercise. Used with _____, heart monitors can save lives.

success *(n.)*

successful *(adj.)*

  4. The new braces are one of the most _____ kinds of spinoff technology. The _____ of the braces is due to the fact that they are clear and effective.

use *(n.)*

useful *(adj.)*

  5. The continuous _____ of freeze-dried food in space is an advantage because it doesn't require refrigeration. This food is also _____ for people who live where there is little or no electricity.

PART 2

Synonyms

Synonyms are words with similar meanings. For example, *anxious* and *worried* are synonyms.

Read each sentence. Write the synonym of the word in parentheses in the space provided. Use each word only once.

alert	buildup	enhance	fascinated
applications	concern	extensive	modify
benefit	dependable		

1. NASA continues to engage in _____ (*lengthy*) research to improve technology for scientific use.

2. If people are ever able to travel to another planet, they will need to _____ (*adapt*) their way of life to an unfamiliar environment.

3. Spinoff products that we use in our homes _____ (*improve*) our everyday lives in many ways.

4. Computers are faster and much more _____ (*reliable*) than they were 30 years ago.

5. Medical products developed from NASA's research _____ (*help*) us all.

6. I am _____ (*intrigued*) by the new computer technology that is being developed.

7. Devices that _____ (*warn*) people of a buildup of carbon monoxide in the air have saved many lives.

8. A(n) _____ (*accumulation*) of carbon dioxide in the home can be toxic.

9. Safety and quality of food is a(n) _____ (*worry*) to people everywhere.

10. Space science has developed many valuable _____ (*uses*) of spinoff technology.

Vocabulary in Context

**Read the following sentences. Complete each sentence with the correct word from the box.
Use each word only once.**

access *(n.)*	eliminated *(v.)*	intense *(adj.)*	superior *(adj.)*
detected *(v.)*	fatigue *(n.)*	scarce *(adj.)*	translucent *(adj.)*
durable *(adj.)*	hazard *(n.)*		

1. Sitting at a desk for a long time can lead to _____, so it's a good idea to get up and walk around a bit every hour.

2. Rain is _____ in that part of the county. As a result, forest fires often occur there.

3. My new laptop is _____ to my old one. It's lighter and faster, and it has more memory, too.

4. Be careful when you walk near my home. The cracked sidewalk in front of my neighbor's

   house is a(n) _____.

5. Even though it's very cold, the sun is very _____. You'll need to wear sunglasses when you go outside today.

6. All students have _____ to the college library with their ID card. They can use it to check out books, too.

7. Carla's backpack is very _____. She's used it for years, and it's still in excellent condition.

8. When Selena _____ smoke in her apartment, she called 911 and alerted her neighbor. Everyone escaped the building safely.

9. My new contact lenses _____ my need for glasses. They're much more comfortable, too.

10. The _____ window allowed a lot of light into the room, but it wasn't clear enough to see through.

Reading Skill

Read the article again. Underline the headings. Then scan the article and complete the following outline, using the headings that you have underlined to help you. You will use this outline later to answer specific questions about the article.

Spinoff Technology: Its Uses in Our Everyday Lives

I.   Introduction _____

    A. _____

    B. _____

    C. This research and technology helps people through spinoff technology. ____

II. _____

    A. A technology originally developed for space; it benefits nations and the world. __

    B. _____

III. Spinoff Technology in Our Homes and Communities _____

    A. _____

    B. _____

    C. Freeze-dried food _____

    D. _____

IV. _____

    A. Medical thermometers that do not touch the body _____

    B. _____

    C. _____

V. _____

    A. _____

    B. *A heart-monitoring device that helps monitor the intensity of exercise*

VI. *Conclusion*

    A. *There are many spinoff products that are useful in our everyday lives.*

    B. _____

Information Recall

Review the information in the outline you have completed. Then answer the questions.

1. Why is spinoff technology important?

_____

_____

2. How can spinoff technology be useful in our homes?

_____

_____

_____

3. How can spinoff technology be helpful in medicine?

_____

_____

_____

4. How can spinoff technology be used in sports?

_____

_____

_____

Writing a Summary

A summary is a short paragraph that provides the most important information in a reading. It usually does not include details, just main ideas. When you write a summary, it is important to use your own words and not copy directly from the reading.

Write a brief summary of the passage. It should not be more than five sentences. Use your own words. Be sure to indent the first line.

Topics for Discussion and Writing

1. Carbon monoxide detectors are common in many American homes. Do you think it's important to have one in your home? What other detectors are important to have? Discuss your ideas with your classmates.

2. Work alone. Arrange the following spinoffs in order of importance to you. Then work with a partner to compare and discuss your lists.

Spinoff Technology	Your Order of Importance	Your Partner's Order of Importance
carbon monoxide detectors		
clothing made of "phase change" materials		
computer mouse		
extended-wear contact lenses		
freeze-dried food		
medical thermometer		
satellite TV		
scratch-resistant lenses		
translucent, ceramic braces		
water filtration system		

3. Write in your journal. What spinoff technology has benefited you the most? Why has it been such an advantage to you? In what ways do you make use of it?

Critical Thinking

1. Even with the advantages of spinoff technology, many people still feel that funding for the study of space should be cut back and the money used for other purposes. Do you agree or disagree? Explain your reasons for your opinion.

2. What technology would you like to see developed from research on space technology? Who do you think it will benefit? Why is this technology important to you?

3. What do you think is the author's purpose in writing this article? Does the author convince you of the importance of funding the study of space? Why or why not?

Crossword Puzzle

Review the words in the box below. Then read the clues on the next page. Write the words in the correct spaces in the puzzle.

affordably	durable	hazards	scarce
applications	eliminate	intense	spinoff
astronomy	extensive	lengthy	superior
buildup	fatigue	moderates	toxic
century	funding	nature	universe
detect	harmless		

Crossword Puzzle Clues

ACROSS CLUES

2. The _____ is everything in outer space: our solar system, the stars, etc.

3. Most people have always been curious about the _____ of outer space. What is it like?

7. The system for cleansing water _____, or inexpensively, benefits people worldwide.

8. There are hundreds of examples of _____ technology that have improved our lives.

11. People cannot sense the _____ of some dangerous gases because they are odorless.

13. _____ is the study of everything outside the earth's atmosphere.

17. Much of technology developed by NASA has many useful _____ in our everyday lives.

19. People have special devices in their homes to _____ smoke and dangerous gases.

20. Many spinoff products are very _____. They do not break easily and last a long time.

21. NASA created contact lenses that are _____ to previous lenses. They are less likely to lead to infection than previous lenses were.

22. NASA developed a way to clean water for people in remote areas where water is _____.

DOWN CLUES

1. A(n) _____ is 100 years.

4. Many space missions are quite _____. They can last for several years.

5. Hand-held thermometers _____ the risk of spreading infection from one person to another.

6. Anything _____ can be deadly.

9. Scientific research is expensive. It requires a lot of _____.

10. Scientists conducted _____ research to develop freeze-dried food that lasts for years.

12. Astronauts encounter many _____, or dangers, during journeys into space.

14. NASA developed material that _____, or controls, temperatures between the body and the environment.

15. In general, carbon dioxide is _____. It is not usually dangerous in open areas.

16. Today's light athletic shoes help reduce runners' _____, so they do not tire so quickly.

18. Running for a long period of time is an example of a(n) _____ activity.

Government and History

Researchers exploring Antarctica

1. What is more important: protecting the environment or providing resources to the world? Can there be a compromise between the two?

2. How can ancient discoveries help us learn about the past?

3. Do you think it is important to learn about the history of a culture or a country? Why or why not? How can knowledge of history help us in the present?

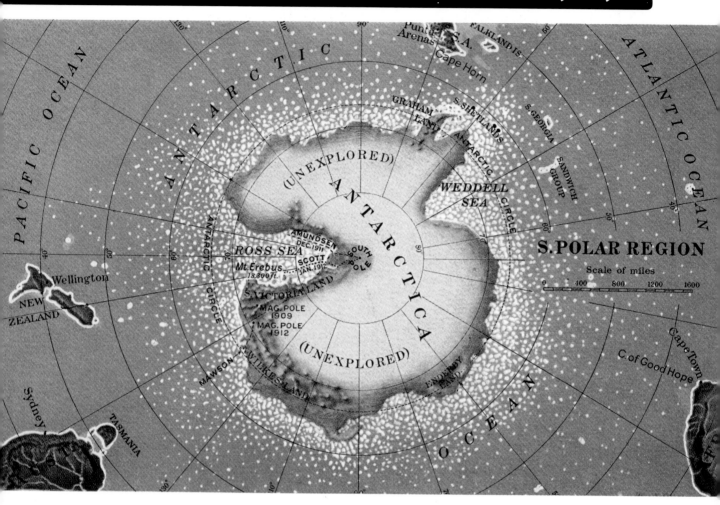

Prereading

1. Where is Antarctica?

2. With a partner, discuss what you know about Antarctica.

3. Some scientists study Antarctica. What are possible reasons why?

4. Look at the title. What do you think this article will discuss about Antarctica? Check (√) all that apply.

_____ a. Animals   _____ d. People
_____ b. Climate   _____ e. Plants
_____ c. Geography   _____ f. Politics

Reading

🎧 **Read the passage carefully. Then complete the exercises that follow.**

CD 2
TR 5

Antarctica: Whose Continent Is It Anyway?
by Daniel and Sally Grotta, *Popular Science*

The *World Discoverer*, our cruise ship, stopped in front of a white ice cliff higher than the ship's mast. As large as France, the Ross Ice Shelf of Antarctica extends unbroken along the Ross Sea for hundreds of miles.

Like other passengers on our cruise ship, we had been lured by an irresistible
5 attraction: the chance to visit the most remote place on Earth, and the most unusual. The coldest place on Earth is also the subject of conflicting interests: scientists, tourists, environmentalists, and oil and mineral seekers.

The Madrid Protocol

Scientists treasure the unparalleled advantages for research; tourists prize the chance to visit Earth's last frontier; environmentalists fear that increases in both
10 activities will pollute the continent and jeopardize its fabulous creatures; others contend that preserving Antarctica as a kind of world park will deprive the rest of the world of much-needed oil and mineral reserves.

Fears of Antarctica's ruin through commercial exploitation was partly reduced by the October, 1991, 31-nation signing of the Madrid Protocol, which bans oil and gas
15 exploration until 2048. But Antarctica's unique attributes—it is the coldest, driest, and highest continent—will keep it at the focus of conflicting scientific and touristic interests.

A Unique Continent

Think of a place as remote as the far side of the moon, as strange as Saturn, and as inhospitable as Mars, and that will give some idea of what Antarctica is like. A mere
20 2.4 percent of its 5.4 million-square-mile land mass is ice-free, and then, only for a few months a year. Scientists estimate that 70 percent of the world's fresh water is locked away in Antarctica's ice cap; if it were ever to melt, sea levels might rise 200 feet.

In Antarctica, winds can blow at better than 200 mph, and temperatures drop as low as minus 128.6°F. There's not a single village or town, not a tree, bush, or blade of
25 grass on the entire continent.

But far from being merely a useless continent, Antarctica is vital to life on Earth. The continent's vast ice fields reflect sunlight back into space, preventing the planet from overheating. The cold water that the breakaway icebergs generate flows north

and mixes with equatorial warm water, producing currents, clouds, and ultimately
30 creating complex weather patterns. Antarctic seas teem with life, making them an
important link in the world food chain. The frigid waters of the Southern Ocean are
home to species of birds and mammals that are found nowhere else.

The National Science Foundation (NSF) is the government agency responsible
for the U.S. stations in Antarctica. Because of the continent's extreme cold and
35 almost complete isolation, the NSF considers it to be the best place to study and
understand such phenomena as temperature circulation in the oceans, unique
animal life, ozone depletion, and glacial history. And buried deep in layers
of Antarctic ice lie clues to ancient climates, clues such as trapped bubbles of
atmospheric gases, which can help predict whether present and future global
40 warming poses a real threat.

The Antarctic Treaty

Until scientists began the first serious study of the continent during the 1957–58
International Geophysical Year (IGY), a multi-country cooperative research project,
Antarctica was dismissed as a vast, useless continent.

Based upon early explorations and questionable land grants, seven countries,
45 including Great Britain, Chile, and Argentina, claim sovereignty over vast tracts of the
continent. However, as IGY wound down, the question of who owns Antarctica came
to a head. The 12 participating countries reached an international agreement, the
Antarctic Treaty, which took effect in June 1961.

The number has since grown, making 48 in all. It established Antarctica as a
50 "continent for science and peace," and temporarily set aside all claims of sovereignty
for as long as the treaty remains in effect.

The rules of the treaty meant that as tourists to Antarctica, passengers on our
cruise ship needed neither passports nor visas. Except for a handful of sites of special
scientific interest, specially protected areas, and specially managed areas, there was
55 nothing to restrict us from wandering anywhere we wanted.

Primarily because of its scientific and ecological importance, many scientists feel
that Antarctica should be dedicated to research only. They feel that tourists should
not be permitted to come. However, recent events have shown that the greatest future
threat to Antarctica may not be tourism or scientific stations, but the worldwide
60 thirst for oil and minerals. "The reason the Antarctic Treaty was negotiated and
went through so quickly," geologist John Splettstoesser explains, "is that at the time,
relatively few minerals were known to exist there."

By the early 1970s, however, there were some indications that there might be gas
and oil in Antarctica. The treaty countries decided that no commercial companies
65 would be permitted to explore for resources. The Madrid Protocol bans all exploration
or commercial exploitation of natural resources on the continent for 50 years.

Like the Antarctic Treaty itself, the Madrid Protocol is binding only on the treaty countries. There's nothing to stop non-treaty countries from establishing commercial bases anywhere on the continent and doing whatever they please.

Latest Developments

70 In February, 2014, China announced its plan for a fourth Antarctic Research base, and plans for a fifth base in the near future. (Japan, Germany, and Italy have five, and Great Britain and the United States have six). For now, mining is prohibited under the Antarctic Treaty, but the treaty will be up for review in 2048. There is a growing concern that countries will then push for mining rights.

75 So whose continent is Antarctica, anyway? Former Vice President Albert Gore best expresses the feelings of those of us who have fallen in love with this strange and spectacular land: "I think that it should be held in trust as a global ecological reserve for all the people of the world, not just in this generation, but later generations to come as well."

Fact Finding

Read the passage again. Then read the following statements. Check (√) whether each statement is True or False. If a statement is false, rewrite it so that it is true. Then go back to the passage and find the line that supports your answer.

1. _____ True _____ False People are interested in Antarctica for a variety of reasons.

_____

2. _____ True _____ False Antarctica is the coldest place on Earth.

_____

3. _____ True _____ False Most of Antarctica is ice-free.

_____

4. _____ True _____ False Antarctica is a useless continent.

_____

5. _____ True _____ False Important information about the past may be buried under the Antarctic ice.

_____

6. _____ True _____ False Thirty-nine countries have agreed to the Antarctic Treaty.

_____

7. _____ True _____ False Many tourists feel that they should be able to visit Antarctica.

_____

8. _____ True _____ False The Madrid Protocol allows countries to explore Antarctica for natural resources.

_____

Reading Analysis

Read each question carefully. Circle the letter or number of the correct answer, or write your answer in the space provided.

   1. Read lines 1–3.

      a. What is the **World Discoverer**?

      _____

      b. Who does **our** refer to?

      _____

      c. What is as large as France?
         1. The *World Discoverer*
         2. The Ross Ice Shelf
         3. Antarctica

   2. Read lines 4–7.

      a. **Lure** means
         1. invite.
         2. visit.
         3. attract.

      b. **Irresistible** means
         1. fascinating.
         2. distant.
         3. unusual.

      c. What is the **irresistible attraction**?

      _____

      d. What follows the **colon (:)**?
         1. Additional information
         2. An example
         3. An explanation

      e. **Remote** means
         1. distant and isolated.
         2. extremely cold.
         3. very unusual.

      f. **Conflicting** means
         1. opposing.
         2. intense.
         3. excited.

g. Which groups are most likely to have conflicting interests?
   1. Scientists and environmentalists
   2. Tourists and scientists
   3. Scientists and oil/mineral seekers
   4. Environmentalists and oil/mineral seekers

3. Read lines 8–12.
   a. **Unparalleled** means
      1. unique.
      2. expensive.
      3. comparable.
   b. **Pollute** means
      1. populate.
      2. contaminate.
      3. popularize.
   c. Who does **others** refer to?
      1. Tourists
      2. Scientists
      3. Environmentalists
      4. Oil and mineral seekers
   d. **Contend** means
      1. ask.
      2. hope.
      3. argue.
   e. **Deprive** means
      1. keep from.
      2. give to.
      3. help with.

4. Read lines 13–15.
   a. **Exploitation** means
      1. misuse.
      2. sale.
      3. travel.
   b. A **ban** is
      1. a conflict.
      2. a prohibition.
      3. an agreement.

5. Read lines 18–21.
   a. **Inhospitable** means
      1. unwelcoming.
      2. distant.
      3. frigid.

b. What does **a mere 2.4 percent** mean?
   1. Approximately 2.4 percent
   2. Exactly 2.4 percent
   3. Only 2.4 percent

6. Read lines 26–32.
   a. **Vital** means
      1. crucial.
      2. useless.
      3. interesting.
   b. **Antarctic seas teem with life.** This sentence means that
      1. the water around Antarctica has very little life.
      2. the water around Antarctica has some life.
      3. the water around Antarctica is full of life.
   c. Which one of the following examples represents a **food chain**?
      1. orange tree → oranges → people
      2. insects → birds → cats
      3. farmer → supermarket → people

7. Read lines 34–37. **Depletion** means
   a. great reduction.
   b. heavy pollution.
   c. temperature change.

8. Read lines 42–48.
   a. What is **IGY**?

   _____

   b. When was Antarctica thought of as a useless continent?
      1. Before IGY
      2. After IGY
   c. **Dismissed** means
      1. rejected.
      2. disliked.
      3. forgotten.
   d. When did scientists begin the first serious study of Antarctica?
      1. Before 1957
      2. 1957–1958
      3. After 1958
   e. "As IGY wound down, the question of who owns Antarctica came to a head." What does **came to a head** mean?
      1. Started a big argument
      2. Grew to a large size
      3. Became very important

f. A **treaty** is
   1. an agreement between two or more countries.
   2. an argument between two or more countries.
   3. a question between two or more countries.

9. Read lines 49–51. What does **sovereignty** mean?
   a. Ownership
   b. Boundaries
   c. Continent

10. Read lines 53–55.
   a. What is **a handful**?
      1. A small number
      2. A large number
   b. Which word is a synonym for **sites**?

   _____

11. Read lines 60–62.
   a. **Negotiated** means
      1. worked on.
      2. thought about.
      3. written down.
   b. When does **at the time** refer to?

   _____

12. Read lines 67–69.
   a. **The Madrid Protocol is binding only on the treaty countries.** This sentence means that
      1. all countries must accept the terms of the Madrid Protocol.
      2. only countries that signed the treaty must accept the terms of the Madrid Protocol.
   b. **Binding** means
      1. acceptable.
      2. obligatory.
      3. recorded.
   c. What are **non-treaty countries**?

   _____

13. Read lines 72–74.
   a. **Up for review** means
      1. the terms of the Atlantic Treaty will remain in effect after 2048.
      2. the terms of the Atlantic Treaty will be examined again in 2048.
      3. the terms of the Atlantic Treaty can never be changed.

    b. **Push for** mining rights means
       1. try to get.
       2. disagree about.
       3. agree with.

14. Read the last paragraph. Who thinks this way about Antarctica?
    a. Only Albert Gore
    b. The authors
    c. Everyone who loves Antarctica

15. What is the main idea of the passage?
    a. Antarctica is a valuable continent that everyone wants to exploit for its minerals.
    b. Antarctica is a valuable continent that many governments are interested in making part of their country.
    c. Antarctica is a valuable continent that some people want to exploit, but that others want to protect and use wisely.

Vocabulary Skills

PART 1

Recognizing Word Forms

In English, some verbs become nouns by adding the suffix *-ion* or *-tion*, for example, *suggest (v.)*, *suggestion (n.)*.

Complete each sentence with the correct word form on the left. Use the correct form of the verb. The nouns may be singular or plural.

reflect *(v.)*   **1.** Antarctica is very important to Earth's climate. The continent's ice fields

reflection *(n.)*   _____ sunlight back into space. This _____

                              prevents our planet from overheating.

reduce *(v.)*   **2.** The signing of the Madrid Protocol _____ some fears that

reduction *(n.)*   Antarctica would be ruined through exploration of its natural resources. This

                              may only be a temporary _____ as the ban on oil and gas

                              will be reviewed in 2048.

deplete *(v.)*

depletion *(n.)*

3. We _____ the world's supply of oil and natural gas at a steady rate. In order to reduce the rate of _____ of these natural resources, we need to resort to alternate sources of energy.

exploit *(v.)*

exploitation *(n.)*

4. The Madrid Protocol prohibits the _____ of oil and gas for profit in Antarctica. In other words, countries are not allowed to _____ the natural resources of the continent.

negotiate *(v.)*

negotiation *(n.)*

5. Nations _____ the Antarctic Treaty very quickly because little was known about the natural resources on the continent. Future _____ , however, are probably going to be more difficult.

PART 2

Synonyms

Synonyms are words with similar meanings. For example, *site* and *area* are synonyms.

Read each sentence. Write the synonym of the word in parentheses in the space provided. Use each word only once.

ban	inhospitable	remote	unparalleled
conflicting	irresistible	treaty	vital
dismissed	lure		

1. Antarctica is the most _____ (*unwelcoming*) continent on Earth. Nothing lives there; nothing grows there.

2. Antarctica is at the very southernmost point of the planet. It is completely _____ (*isolated*) from every other continent.

3. Visiting a continent where no one lives, where no trees or plants grow, and where the weather is the coldest on Earth is a(n) _____ (*fascinating*) idea.

4. It is understandable that environmentalists and mineral seekers would have _____ (*opposing*) views on how Antarctica should be developed.

5. It would be wonderful if all countries signed a(n) _____ (*agreement*) that would help protect the Antarctic environment.

6. The conditions that exist in Antarctica are _____ (*unique*) in all the world. No other country has conditions that compare to Antarctica's.

7. Like Antarctica, Alaska was once _____ (*rejected*) as a useless region—until gold was discovered there.

8. The vast areas of ice on Antarctica are _____ (*crucial*) to maintaining the planet's temperature so it doesn't become too hot.

9. Some people worry that the _____ (*prohibition*) on mining may be in danger after 2048 under the conditions of the Madrid Protocol.

10. Many people visit Antarctica. The _____ (*attraction*) of visiting such a huge, unusual, and isolated place is fascinating to them.

Vocabulary in Context

Read the following sentences. Complete each sentence with the correct word or phrase from the box. Use each word or phrase only once.

contends *(v.)*	exploit *(v.)*	negotiated *(v.)*	pushed for *(v.)*
depletion *(n.)*	handful *(n.)*	pollute *(v.)*	reflected *(v.)*
deprived *(v.)*	mere *(adj.)*		

1. Many people ride bikes instead of driving cars because bicycles don't _____ the air the way that most other kinds of transportation do.

2. The little girl was fascinated at the way her face was _____ in the lake's water.

3. Marc and I disagree about where to raise our children. He _____ that living in the city is the best place for all of us, but I think the country is the best.

4. My brother _____ a lower price when he bought a used car from a dealer. The original price seemed too high.

5. Only a _____ of students attended the party. Most of the other students were busy studying for the exam.

6. The workers' union representative _____ with management for higher wages and more vacation time.

7. There was very little rain this year. We are very concerned about the _____ of the fresh water supply in our area.

8. When I was a child, my parents always _____ me of dessert. I wasn't allowed to eat any sweet things until I was older.

9. Because Cindy lives a _____ three blocks from school, she can get to her classes in just a few minutes.

10. Many people believe that traditional zoos _____ animals by keeping them in cages.

Reading Skill

Using Headings to Create an Outline

Readings often have headings that introduce new ideas, topics, or details. Using headings to make an outline can help you understand and remember the most important information from a reading.

Read the article again. Underline the headings. Then scan the article and complete the following outline, using the sentences that you have underlined to help you. You will use this outline later to answer specific questions about the article.

I. People with Conflicting Interests in Antarctica _____

    A. Scientists _____

        Reason: _____

    B. _____

        Reason: They prize the chance to visit Earth's last frontier. _____

    C. Oil and Mineral Seekers _____

        Reason: _____

II. The Madrid Protocol

    A. Date: _____

    B. Original number of participating nations: _____

    C. Purpose: _____

III. Antarctica Is Vital to Life on Earth. _____

    A. _____

    B. _____

    C. Southern Ocean is home to unique animals. _____

IV. _____

    A. Establish Antarctica as a continent for science and peace _____

    B. _____

    C. _____

V. _____

    A. China announced plans for a fifth base next year. _____

    B. _____

Information Recall

Read each question carefully. Use the outline to answer the questions. Do not refer back to the text.

1. Why are there conflicting interests regarding Antarctica?

    _____

    _____

2. What is the Madrid Protocol?

    _____

    _____

3. Is Antarctica necessary to life on Earth? Why or why not?

_____

_____

4. What is the purpose of the Atlantic Treaty?

_____

_____

5. What is the future of Antarctica?

_____

_____

Writing a Summary

A summary is a short paragraph that provides the most important information in a reading. It usually does not include details, just main ideas. When you write a summary, it is important to use your own words and not copy directly from the reading.

Write a brief summary of the passage. It should not be more than five sentences. Use your own words. Be sure to indent the first line.

_____

_____

_____

_____

_____

_____

Topics for Discussion and Writing

1. The authors ask who Antarctica belongs to. Whose continent *is* Antarctica? Do you think it should belong to one country, many countries, or to no one? Write a composition explaining your opinion.

2. In this passage, the authors say that tourists consider Antarctica to be Earth's last frontier. However, other people do not agree with this statement. They believe that there are other places on Earth that have not yet been fully explored and that are still exciting, challenging places to go to. Alone, or with a partner, decide what other such places exist on Earth and examine why people would be interested in going there.

3. Write in your journal. The authors describe Antarctica by comparing it with other places and by giving facts about it. The authors are trying to convey an image and a feeling about this unusual continent. Imagine that you are visiting Antarctica. Write a journal entry in which you describe what you see and how being in Antarctica makes you feel. Do you have feelings similar to those of the first explorers?

Critical Thinking

1. According to this passage, scientists estimate that 70 percent of the world's fresh water is locked away in Antarctica's ice cap; if it were ever to melt, sea levels might rise 200 feet. What do you think would happen if sea levels rose 200 feet?

2. When the Antarctic Treaty was signed in 1961, very little was known about the continent's natural resources. What does John Splettstoesser believe about the relationship between the quick signing of the treaty and the lack of information about the resources? In other words, why was the treaty signed so quickly?

3. Scientists, tourists, environmentalists, and oil and mineral seekers all have different opinions about what to do with Antarctica. Choose one of these four groups and imagine that you are a member. Working with a partner or in a small group, make a list of reasons why Antarctica is important to your particular group. Compare your list with your classmates' lists. Then as a class, decide which group has the strongest reasons to support its point of view.

4. Form a panel of experts. Write a set of guidelines for the protection and use of Antarctica by all the interested countries of the world. You want to be fair to all the interested countries. You also want to try to satisfy the four groups previously mentioned: scientists, environmentalists, tourists, and oil and mineral seekers.

Crossword Puzzle

Review the words in the box below. Then read the clues on the next page. Write the words in the correct spaces in the puzzle.

ban	dismissed	lured	sites
binding	exploitation	mere	sovereignty
conflicting	handful	negotiated	treaty
contend	inhospitable	pollute	unparalleled
depletion	irresistible	remote	vital
deprive			

Crossword Puzzle Clues

ACROSS CLUES

3. It is _____ to protect Antarctica. This continent is essential to life on Earth.

9. Several nations claim _____ over parts of Antarctica, but ownership is under debate.

11. Antarctica has many _____, or locations, of special scientific interest.

13. The possible _____ of any resources in Antarctica must be carefully limited.

14. The authors were _____ to Antarctica because it is so distant and so unusual.

15. Environmentalists worry that oil companies will _____ Antarctica if they are allowed access.

17. Antarctica is the most _____ place on Earth. It is even more distant than Australia.

18. There are only a(n) _____ of locations in Antarctica that are of special interest to any tourists.

19. According to the Antarctic _____, people do not need passports or visas to visit Antarctica.

20. Like Antarctica, Alaska was once _____ as a useless territory.

21. Many people have _____ interests in Antarctica. They do not agree at all.

DOWN CLUES

1. Hopefully, the _____ against the exploitation of natural resources in Antarctica will continue.

2. The Antarctic Treaty was _____ very quickly and took effect in 1961.

4. As the coldest place on Earth, Antarctica is very _____. No one can live there.

5. Scientists worry about the _____ of the ozone layer over Antarctica because it protects the earth.

6. Although Antarctica is vast, a(n) _____ 2.4 percent of it is not covered by ice.

7. A written agreement is only _____ on the people or countries that sign it.

8. Antarctica offers scientists _____, or unique, opportunities for research.

10. Oil and mineral seekers feel that no one should _____ the world of Antarctica's resources.

12. Because Antarctica is such an unusual place, the authors found the idea of visiting it to be _____.

16. Oil and mineral seekers _____ that the world needs the reserves in Antarctica.

Prereading

1. Do you think it's important to learn about humans of the past? Why or why not?

2. What are some ways we can learn about humans of the past?

3. Read the title of this article and look at the photo. Who is the messenger from the past? What message, or information, can he give us today?

Reading

🎧 **Read the passage carefully. Then complete the exercises that follow.**

The Mystery of the Iceman

The discovery of the Iceman in 1991 was an unprecedented event. A well-preserved body thousands of years old could provide a wealth of information never available before. In their excitement, scientists rushed to examine the body and its belongings. Twenty years later, a more complete investigation resulted in new discoveries and
5 some surprising information.

The Discovery: A Messenger from the Past
by James Shreeve, *Discover*

His people said good-bye and watched him walk off toward the mountains. They had little reason to fear for his safety: the man was well dressed in insulated clothing and equipped with tools needed to survive the Alpine climate. However, as weeks passed without his return, they must have grown worried, then anxious, and finally
10 resigned. After many years everyone who knew him had died, and not even a memory of the man remained.

Then, on an improbably distant day, he came down from the mountain. Things had changed a bit: it wasn't the Bronze Age anymore, and he was a celebrity. When a melting glacier released its hold on a 4,000-year-old corpse in September 1991, it was
15 quite rightly called one of the most important archaeological finds of the century.

Discovered by a German couple hiking at 10,500 feet in the Italian Tyrol near the Austrian border, the partially freeze-dried body still wore remnants of leather garments and boots that had been stuffed with straw for insulation. The hikers alerted scientists from the University of Innsbruck in Austria, whose more complete
20 examination revealed that the man was tattooed on his back and behind his knee. At his side was a bronze ax of a type typical in southern central Europe around 2000 B.C. On his expedition—perhaps to hunt or to search for metal ore—he had also carried an all-purpose stone knife, a wooden backpack, a bow and a quiver, a small bag containing a flint lighter and kindling, and an arrow repair kit in a leather pouch.

25 Such everyday gear gives an unprecedented perspective on life in early Bronze Age Europe. "The most exciting thing is that we genuinely appear to be looking at a man who had some kind of accident in the course of a perfectly ordinary trip," says archaeologist Ian Kinnes of the British Museum. "These are not artifacts placed in a grave, but the man's own possessions."

30 The Iceman and his countrymen lived in a society built around small, stable villages. He may well have been hunting when he died. X-rays of the quiver showed that it contained 14 arrows. While his backpack was empty, careful exploration of the trench where he died revealed remnants of animal skin and bones at the same spot where the pack lay. There was also the remainder of a pile of berries. Clearly the man
35 didn't starve to death.

So why did the Iceman die? The trench provided him with shelter from the elements. Furthermore, he had a braided mat of grass to keep him warm. If injury or illness caused the Iceman's death, an autopsy on the 4,000-year-old victim could turn up some clues.

40 Archaeologist Colin Renfrew of Cambridge University says, "It may be possible to get very long DNA sequences out of this material. This is far and away the most exciting aspect of the discovery."

For the time being, all biological research has literally been put on ice at the University of Innsbruck while an international team of experts, led by researcher
45 Konrad Spindler, figures out a way to thaw the body without destroying it. As sensational as it sounds, it remains to be seen how useful 4,000-year-old human DNA will really be. "The problem is that we are dealing with a single individual," says evolutionary biologist Robert Sokal of the State University of New York at Stony Brook. "In order to make statements about the population that existed at the time, we
50 need more specimens."

The wish for more messengers from the past may yet come true. The Iceman's return has demonstrated that the local climate is warmer now than it has been for 4,000 years. People are beginning to wonder—and plan for—what the melting ice may reveal next.

The Examination: Iceman Autopsy: Unfrozen
by Stephen S. Hall, *National Geographic*

55 On a November day in 2010, two men opened the door of the Iceman's chamber in the South Tyrol Museum of Archaeology in Bolzano, Italy. One of the men was a young scientist named Marco Samadelli.

With Samadelli was a local pathologist named Eduard Egarter Vigl. A handful of other scientists and doctors gathered around, preparing to defrost the Iceman. The
60 next day they would perform the first full-scale autopsy on the thawed body, hoping to shed new light on the mystery of who the Iceman really was and how he had died such a violent death.

This was not the first time that the Iceman had been subject to intense scientific scrutiny. The most astonishing revelation came in 2001, when a local radiologist
65 named Paul Gostner noticed a detail that had been overlooked in the images: an arrowhead buried in the Iceman's left shoulder, indicating that he had been shot

from behind. The oldest accidentally preserved human ever found was the victim of a brutal murder. Scientists theorized that enemies had an argument with the Iceman, chased him, and caught up with him on the mountain, where the body was discovered more than 5,000 years later.

It was a good story that fit the evidence—until Gostner took a closer look at the Iceman's stomach, which appeared to be full. If he was right, it meant the Iceman had eaten a large meal minutes before his death—not the sort of thing someone being chased by armed enemies would likely do.

"Gostner told us he thought the stomach was full," said Albert Zink, director of the EURAC Institute for Mummies and the Iceman in Bolzano. After further thought, Zink and his colleagues drew up a more ambitious plan: a head-to-toe investigation.

The autopsy took about nine hours; analysis of the material that the scientists found will take years. The first revelations were disclosed in June 2011. From his genes, we now know that the Iceman had brown hair as well as brown eyes. The autopsy results have also rewritten the story of the Iceman's final moments. DNA analysis of the final meal is ongoing, but initial tests indicate the presence of meat of a kind of wild goat. "He really must have had a heavy meal at the end," Zink said. It appears he was resting in a spot protected from the wind, peacefully digesting his meal, unaware of the danger he was in. And of course, unaware of the intense attention awaiting him far in the future.

the Iceman's dagger

the Iceman's ax

Fact Finding

Read the passage again. Then read the following statements. Check (√) whether each statement is True or False. If a statement is false, rewrite it so that it is true. Then go back to the passage and find the line that supports your answer.

1. _____ True _____ False   The year 1991 was the first time a well-preserved body from thousands of years ago was discovered.

_____

2. _____ True _____ False   The Iceman was discovered in Europe by scientists.

_____

3. _____ True _____ False   At first, scientists weren't sure how the Iceman had died.

_____

4. _____ True _____ False   Scientists learned nothing from the Iceman's possessions.

_____

5. _____ True _____ False   In 2010, scientists performed an autopsy on the Iceman.

_____

6. _____ True _____ False   Scientists obtained genetic information from the Iceman's body.

_____

7. _____ True _____ False   We do not know what the Iceman looked like.

_____

8. _____ True _____ False   Scientists believe that the Iceman was murdered.

_____

Reading Analysis

Read each question carefully. Circle the number or letter of the correct answer, or write your answer in the space provided.

1. Read lines 1–3.

a. **Well-preserved** means
1. frozen.
2. hidden.
3. protected.

b. What was **the well-preserved body**?

_____

2. Read lines 6–8.

a. **Insulated** clothing
1. is very bright and colorful.
2. has something added to it to provide warmth.
3. is made of some kind of leather.

b. **Survive** means
1. continue to live.
2. walk in the mountains.
3. find one's way.

3. Read lines 12–15.

a. The first sentence means
1. the Iceman walked down from the mountain.
2. the Iceman woke up on the mountain.
3. the Iceman's body was brought down from the mountain.

b. What does the **4,000-year-old corpse** refer to?

_____

4. Read lines 16–20.

a. **Remnants** are
1. shirts.
2. small pieces.
3. tools.

b. **Garments** refers to
1. clothing.
2. weapons.
3. food.

c. **Alerted** means
1. frightened.
2. notified.
3. prepared.

d. **Whose** refers to
1. the Iceman.
2. the scientists.
3. the hikers.

5. Read lines 23–26.

a. What are some examples of the Iceman's **everyday gear**?

_____

b. **Gear** means
1. equipment.
2. weapons.

c. If something is **unprecedented**,
1. it is frightening.
2. it is dangerous.
3. it never happened before.

d. A **perspective** is
1. a point of view.
2. a way of life.
3. a type of metal.

6. Read lines 31–35.

a. **He may well have been hunting** means
1. he was definitely hunting.
2. he was usually hunting.
3. he was probably hunting.

b. What does **clearly** mean?
1. Unfortunately
2. Obviously
3. Possibly

7. Read lines 36–39.

a. **Elements** means
1. weather conditions.
2. injury and illness.
3. enemies.

b. What follows **furthermore**?
  1. An example
  2. A theory
  3. Additional information
c. An **autopsy** is
  1. a report on an investigation.
  2. an examination on a body.
  3. a description of an injury or illness.

8. In line 41, **far and away** indicates
   a. distance.
   b. importance.
   c. excitement.

9. Read lines 43–45.
   a. **For the time being** means
     1. for a long time.
     2. for now.
     3. for a human being.
   b. **Put on ice** is an idiom. It means
     1. finished.
     2. put in a different place.
     3. postponed.
   c. **Literally** means
     1. something is written as literature.
     2. something is carefully done.
     3. something means exactly what it says.
   d. How was the research **literally** put on ice?
     1. The research was delayed for a time.
     2. The Iceman was kept frozen.
     3. Winter began in Austria.

10. In line 51, **yet** means
    a. still.
    b. not.
    c. soon.

11. Read lines 58–62.
    a. **Defrost** means
      1. to freeze.
      2. to thaw.
      3. to open.

b. **To shed new light** means
  1. to get a new understanding.
  2. to reject the old evidence.
  3. to do a new examination.

c. **Violent** means
  1. peaceful.
  2. brutal.
  3. sudden.

12. Read lines 64–70.
  a. An **astonishing revelation** is
    1. a different result.
    2. an interesting event.
    3. a surprising discovery.

  b. What was the astonishing revelation?
    1. The Iceman was 5,000 years old.
    2. The Iceman had been murdered.
    3. The Iceman had been closely examined.

  c. **Theorize** means
    1. to make an educated guess.
    2. to question if something is true.
    3. to look for an answer.

13. Read lines 79–80.
  a. **Disclosed** means
    1. understood.
    2. revealed.
    3. discovered.

  b. **As well as** means
    1. as good as.
    2. with.
    3. and.

14. What is the main idea of the passage?
  a. Archaeologists must carefully thaw the Iceman in order to study his DNA.
  b. The discovery of the Iceman has given us important information about how people lived thousands of years ago.
  c. As temperatures around the world become warmer, more bodies from a long time ago may begin to be discovered.

Vocabulary Skills

PART 1

Recognizing Word Forms

In English, the noun and verb forms of some words are the same, for example, *promise (v.)*, *promise (n.)*.

Read each sentence. Write the correct word form on the left. Use the correct form of the verbs, in either the affirmative or the negative. In addition, indicate whether you are using the verb or the noun form by circling *(v.)* or *(n.)*.

alert
1. The hikers _____ the scientists at the university after they
   (v.) / (n.)

   discovered the Iceman's body. The scientists responded to the

   _____ immediately.
   (v.) / (n.)

release
2. When the glacier melted, it _____ the 4,000-year-old
   (v.) / (n.)

   corpse. This _____ was a very important event in the
   (v.) / (n.)

   field of archaeology.

damage
3. The hot TV lights _____ some of the tissues in the Iceman's
   (v.) / (n.)

   body. Scientists were not able to examine all of the genetic information

   because of this _____ .
   (v.) / (n.)

repair
4. The Iceman _____ his arrows using the tools in his pouch.
   (v.) / (n.)

   The _____ of his weapons was important to his survival.
   (v.) / (n.)

return
5. The Iceman's people must have been worried when he _____ to his
   (v.) / (n.)

   home. They may have waited for his _____ for several weeks.
   (v.) / (n.)

PART 2

Understanding Useful Phrases

Certain phrases and combinations of words are very common in English. It's important to understand the meaning of these word combinations. *As well as, have little reason to, far and away, for the time being,* and *in the course of* are examples of these useful phrases.

First, match each phrase with the correct meaning. Then complete each sentence with the correct phrase. Use the simple past form if necessary, and use each phrase only once.

_____ 1. as well as   a. also

_____ 2. far and away   b. during; while

_____ 3. for the time being   c. by a very great amount

_____ 4. have little reason to   d. not much cause

_____ 5. in the course of   e. temporarily

1. The Iceman's family _____ worry about his safety. He had warm clothes and tools when he left home.

2. Archaeologist Ian Kinnes believed that the Iceman had an accident

_____ a regular day.

3. Archaeologist Colin Renfrew believed that getting DNA from the Iceman would be

_____ the most important part of the discovery.

4. The circumstances of the Iceman's death may have preserved proof of how he died,

_____ details of his life.

5. _____ , further biological research must wait until an international team of experts finds a safe way to thaw the body.

Vocabulary in Context

Read the following sentences. Complete each sentence with the correct word or phrase from the box. Use each word or phrase only once.

alerted *(v.)*	for the time being	revelation *(n.)*	unprecedented *(adj.)*
clearly *(adv.)*	gear *(n.)*	survive *(v.)*	violent *(adj.)*
disclose *(v.)*	remnants *(n.)*		

1. Neil Armstrong's walk on the moon in 1969 was _____. No one had ever stepped onto the moon's surface before.

2. Peter and his wife just had triplets! _____, they're going to need to move to a larger apartment.

3. Emily is living with her cousin _____. Next week, she is going to move into her own apartment by herself.

4. My parents never allowed me to play _____ video games when I was a child. They only let me play educational ones.

5. Everyone who watched the movie was shocked by the _____ of the murderer's identify. It was quite a surprise to all of us!

6. Diane _____ the fire department when she saw smoke coming from an empty building.

7. After the tornado struck the small town, some people found only _____ of their homes. Fortunately, no one was hurt.

8. The instructor did not _____ information about the final exam until a few days before the test. The students were upset because they needed more time to study.

9. It's impossible for a person to _____ for more than a week without water.

10. When I go hiking, I always put a knife, a flashlight, a camera, and other _____ in my backpack.

Reading Skill

Creating an Information Chart

Creating a chart to compare information on the same topic from two different sources can be very useful. It can highlight first findings with later work, revise previous theories or information, and show what new information is uncovered.

Read the article again, and write the information for the initial discovery and the more recent autopsy in the chart below.

	Original Information (Source): A Messenger from the Past—*Discover*	Recent Information (Source): Iceman Autopsy—*National Geographic*
When the Iceman lived		
The age the Iceman lived in		
The Iceman's equipment		
The Iceman's physical condition		
The marks on the Iceman's body		
The contents of the Iceman's stomach		
The cause of the Iceman's death		
Other information		

Information Recall

Read each question carefully. Use your chart to answer the questions. Do not refer back to the text.

1. What was the Iceman wearing when he was first found?

   _____

   _____

   _____

2. What did the Iceman have with him?

   _____

   _____

   _____

3. What might he have been doing before he died?

   _____

   _____

   _____

4. Describe the findings of the autopsy performed in 2010.

   _____

   _____

   _____

5. What did the autopsy reveal that was unknown when the Iceman was first discovered?

   _____

   _____

   _____

Writing a Summary

A summary is a short paragraph that provides the most important information in a reading. It usually does not include details, just main ideas. When you write a summary, it is important to use your own words and not copy directly from the reading.

Write a brief summary of the passage. It should not be more than five sentences. Use your own words. Be sure to indent the first line.

Topics for Discussion and Writing

1. According to Robert Sokal, an evolutionary biologist at the State University of New York at Stony Brook, we need to find many examples of preserved people from thousands of years ago in order to "make statements about the population that existed at the time." What information do you think we can learn from such discoveries? How might this information be useful to us in the twenty-first century?

2. If you could ask the Iceman questions about himself and his time, what would you ask? Work with a partner, and make a list of questions. Compare your list with your classmates' lists.

3. Write in your journal. Imagine that you were the Iceman 5,000 years ago. Describe your last week alive. Write about what you did, where you went, the people you met, and your last hours.

Critical Thinking

1. In the first paragraph, the author gives a personalized description of what happened to the Iceman thousands of years ago and how his friends and family may have felt about his loss. What do you think the tone or feeling of this paragraph is? How is the tone and style different from the rest of the article? Why do you think the author started the article in this way?

2. What do James Shreeve, the author of the first article, and the scientists quoted in the passage believe about the discovery of the Iceman? What makes you think this is their opinion? Give examples from the passage to support your answer.

3. According to the most recent research, the Iceman lived over 5,000 years ago in the Bronze Age. His society was very different from the civilizations of Egypt and Mesopotamia of the same time period. Select an area of the world, perhaps your own. Refer to the chart below. In pairs or small groups, select one of the ages and find out what characterizes each age. Then refer to the Internet, a history book or an encyclopedia, or your own knowledge. What age best describes the society you chose? Write a description of what life was like 5,000 years ago for the people in the society you have chosen. Discuss how their lives and the lives of the Iceman and his people were similar and how they were different.

Ages of Mankind*

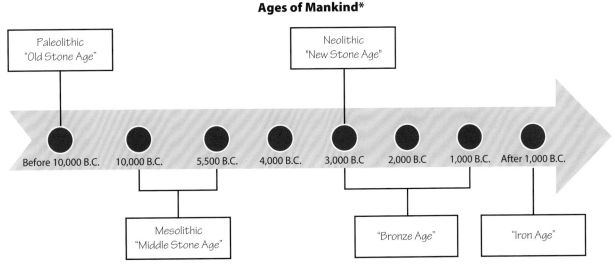

* These ages are approximate, and vary in different parts of the world.

Crossword Puzzle

Review the words in the box below. Then read the clues on the next page. Write the words in the correct spaces in the puzzle.

alerted	elements	insulated	survive
astonishing	everyday	perspective	thaw
clearly	furthermore	preserved	theorize
corpse	garments	remnants	unprecedented
disclosed	gear	revelation	yet

Crossword Puzzle Clues

ACROSS CLUES

1. When the scientists took the frozen man into a warm room, he began to _____.

5. The Iceman's clothing was _____ with straw, or dried grass, which helped keep him warm.

7. Archeologists reconstructed the Iceman's clothing using the _____ he wore.

10. Glaciers worldwide are melting, so scientists may _____ make another fascinating discovery.

12. The Iceman's clothing and equipment provide us with a rare _____ on European life 5,000 years ago.

13. A _____ is a dead body.

15. Humans can _____ for days without food or water but only moments without air.

18. Scientists have an understanding of how the Iceman lived. _____, they have an idea of how he died.

19. Finding an ancient body, with ancient equipment, was a(n) _____ and exciting discovery.

20. The Iceman had food with him. _____, he did not starve to death.

DOWN CLUES

2. The finding of the Iceman's body was a(n) _____ discovery!

3. The Iceman wore warm clothes to protect him from the _____.

4. The Iceman's _____, or clothing, had been made to protect him from severe weather.

6. The first findings from the in-depth examination of the body were _____ in 2011.

8. The autopsy of the Iceman enabled scientists to _____ about his life.

9. Finding an arrowhead in the Iceman's shoulder was a very surprising _____.

11. The dry, frozen environment _____ the Iceman's body very well, including his inner organs.

14. The Iceman was carrying _____ equipment that he usually needed for his daily activities.

16. When the hikers discovered a body in the ice, they _____ scientists at a university.

17. The Iceman's _____ included a bow, arrows, and an ax.

The United States Congress in session

Prereading

1. The United States was not always an independent nation. How did it become one?

2. What kind of government does the United States have? What do you know about this type of government?

3. What is a **constitution**? Why do governments have constitutions? What is their usual purpose?

Reading

🎧 **Read the following passage carefully. Then complete the exercises that follow.**
CD 2
TR 7

The Federal System of Government
by Patricia C. Acheson, excerpted from
Our Federal Government: How It Works

What is the government of the United States exactly? How and when did it come to be? Who were the people who agreed to accept our government and why did they want to accept it?

The answers to these questions lie in the events that took place between 1775 and
5   1787. In 1775, the war against British domination began. At that point, there was no
central American government established by law. There was only the Continental
Congress made up of men who believed in independence and who were willing to
fight for their cause. It was that Congress that declared the colonies independent of
Great Britain in July 1776, and it was only after that decision that the evolution of our
10   present form of government began. The initial step was to establish legal governments
in the states to replace colonial[1] rule. The states established republics; each of the
thirteen new states had elected governors and representative assemblies.

The Continental Congress was without legal foundation, and it was necessary to
establish some form of overall government agreed to by the people and speaking
15   for all the states. However, the Americans of this period reluctantly accepted this
necessity, as the majority believed that they could guarantee their freedom only if
each state remained almost entirely independent of the others.

Therefore, the first government of the United States under the Articles of
Confederation adopted in 1781 was very restricted in its authority. It consisted of a
20   Congress made up of representatives from the states. There was no president with
certain specific powers, only a chairman whose job it was to preside and to keep order.
The Congress had very little power to do anything. Congress could not pass tax laws; it
did not have the sole authority to coin money for use by the states, nor could it regulate
trade between the states. Because it had no money of its own, the Congress could not
25   pay any of its debts, it could not borrow money, and it could not pay an army or a navy.

Within four years after the end of the war in 1783, it became obvious that the system
of government under the Articles of Confederation was not working out. The discontent
and the fact that the new nation was extraordinarily weak without an adequate army or
navy made thoughtful people realize that a better government must be worked out if
30   the United States of America was to be a strong and rich nation. In Philadelphia in 1787,
a convention, or meeting, was held in order to reshape the government. It was there that
our present system of government was born, and the Constitution of the United States
was written. The people of the United States are still governed today by the framework
drawn up in that document over two hundred years ago.

The Constitution
35   The foreword (introduction) to the Constitution stated the democratic principles to
be followed by the United States government. The government must ensure freedom
for the citizens of the United States for all time.

To create such a government was not an easy thing to do. Remember that in
1787 the men at the convention in Philadelphia were pioneers in the setting up of a
40   democratic republican government. They really only knew what they did not want.

---

[1] **Colonial** refers to a colony, or an area that is under the control of a country, and is usually not near that country.

They did not want a king, and they did not want too strong a central government because they were afraid of losing their own freedoms. They certainly wanted to keep the states as they were. To erase them would have been impossible. Each colony had its own individuality and pride. There could be no question of making

45 just one government and forgetting the individual states. Many people were concerned that power would fall into the wrong hands if a strong central government were established. On the other hand, the men in Philadelphia knew that the first government set up under the Articles of Confederation had had too little power to carry out its business, and no one had been satisfied.

50 Here was a dilemma. On the one hand, it seemed that a strong central government was very undesirable because it might endanger the people's liberties. On the other hand, a weak central government had proven inadequate. The solution these men found is called the "system of checks and balances," and it is the heart and soul of the Constitution.

The System of Checks and Balances

55 The writers of the Constitution wanted to make sure that the people's rights would always be safe and that the central or federal government would never become too powerful. A government ought to have three major powers: to make laws, to carry out those laws, and to provide justice under law for the best interests of the people. If these three functions were in the hands of one person or one group, there would

60 be great danger that that person or group could use the power for personal profit rather than for the people. To guard against this possibility, the Constitution provided for three major branches of government: the legislature, or Congress, to make laws; the executive to carry out the laws; and the judiciary to watch over the rights of the people as described in the Constitution. The three branches of the government must

65 work hand in hand.

The powers of these three branches of the government are described carefully in the Constitution. To make sure that the government would never take more power than it was granted in the Constitution, it was carefully stated that any power not given to the government should forever belong to the states. Another reason for

70 describing carefully the powers of the three branches was to prevent any one branch from becoming stronger than the others. Each job in the running of the country was balanced between the legislative, the executive, and the judicial branches. Each part of the government can only function in relation to the others. This system not only balances power between the three branches, but also provides a check on each branch

75 by the others. A good example of the check system can be found in the manner in which laws become laws. The legislature, or Congress, has the job of drafting laws for the country. Once a bill[2] has been passed by the two houses, the Senate and the House

---

[2] A **bill** is the name given to a proposed law before it is signed by the president.

of Representatives, Congress must send a copy to the chief executive, the president of the United States, for his approval. He then has several options as to what he may do. For instance, he may agree with the bill and sign the copy, in which case the law goes into effect. Or, if he should feel that it is not a good law, he may veto it. Vetoing means that he refuses to sign. Should he do that, the copy is returned to the house of Congress in which it originated. If Congress, sure that the proposed law is a necessary one, passes it again by a two-thirds majority, the bill becomes a law regardless of the president's veto. The people are represented in Congress, and if they still favor the law, it is more democratic that they should have it.

The checks system goes further. The judicial branch has its say about the laws of the land. Once Congress and the president have agreed upon a law, it must be enforced all over the United States. If someone disagrees with a federal law and challenges it by disobeying it, the case is brought into the court system of the United States. If the Supreme Court decides to hear the case, it has the duty of examining the law and determining if it is constitutional, or in other words, whether the law is in keeping with the rights of the people as outlined in the Constitution.

This system of balanced power and of checks between the branches of the government means that at all times the people's rights and interests are being carefully guarded. They are in safe hands. It must be stressed, however, that as Thomas Jefferson[3] said, "Eternal vigilance is the price of liberty," and if the people of the United States, their elected representatives, and their judges are not constantly vigilant, no mere words on paper are going to protect their freedom.

---

[3] **Thomas Jefferson** was the principal writer of the Declaration of Independence and the third president of the United States.

The United States Capitol Building

Fact Finding

Read the passage again. Then read the following statements. Check (√) whether each statement is True or False. If a statement is false, rewrite it so that it is true. Then go back to the passage and find the line that supports your answer.

1. _____ True _____ False   The United States became independent in 1775.

_____

2. _____ True _____ False   The first U.S. government did not have a president.

_____

3. _____ True _____ False   The United States' present government began in 1787.

_____

4. _____ True _____ False   The U.S. Constitution described two branches of the government: the legislative and the judicial.

_____

5. _____ True _____ False   The system of checks and balances prevents one branch of government from becoming too powerful.

_____

6. _____ True _____ False   If the president disagrees with a new bill, it can never become a law.

_____

Reading Analysis

Read each question carefully. Circle the letter or number of the correct answer, or write your answer in the space provided.

1. Read lines 5–11.
    a. Which word is a synonym for **domination**?
        1. Rule
        2. War
        3. Government

b. These synonyms mean
 1. protection.
 2. control.
 3. fighting.

c. What does **at that point** mean?
 1. 1775
 2. 1787
 3. Between 1775 and 1787

d. What was the men's **cause**?
 1. War with Britain
 2. Independence from Britain
 3. Creation of a central government

e. A **cause** is
 1. motivation for doing something.
 2. anger at another person or country.
 3. desire for new laws.

f. What does **that Congress** refer to?

_____

g. **Initial** means
 1. a letter of the alphabet.
 2. the first.
 3. the most difficult.

h. **The initial step was to establish legal governments in the states to replace colonial rule.** This sentence means that the people wanted to
 1. start new governments instead of the colonial government.
 2. establish the colonial government again.
 3. get rid of all forms of government.

2. Read lines 13–17.

a. **The Continental Congress was without legal foundation . . . .** This sentence means that
 1. the Continental Congress broke the law.
 2. the Continental Congress did not make laws.
 3. the Continental Congress had no legal authority.

b. **Foundation** means
 1. basis or authority.
 2. independence or freedom.
 3. agreement or understanding.

c. **Reluctantly** means
 1. recently.
 2. unanimously.
 3. unwillingly.

d. Complete the following sentence:
   Gary wanted to find a job in New York because he thinks it is an exciting city. When he was unable to find a job there, he reluctantly
   1. took a job in New Jersey.
   2. continued looking for a job.

e. **Majority** means
   1. some of the people.
   2. more than half of the people.
   3. all of the people.

3. Read lines 18–25.
   a. **Therefore** means
      1. furthermore.
      2. in addition.
      3. as a result.
   b. **Whose** refers to
      1. the president.
      2. the chairman.
      3. the Congress.
   c. What powers did the Continental Congress **not** have? Check (√) all that apply.
      _____ 1. Declare a war
      _____ 2. Borrow from foreign governments
      _____ 3. Coin money for states to use
      _____ 4. Sign treaties
      _____ 5. Regulate trade between the states
      _____ 6. Appoint foreign ambassadors
      _____ 7. Pass tax laws

4. Read lines 27–31.
   a. **Discontent** means
      1. discomfort.
      2. disagreement.
      3. dissatisfaction.
   b. Why did many people feel such discontent with the government?

   _____

   c. In this paragraph, a synonym for **convention** is

   _____ .

   d. In this context, **reshape** means
      1. give a different outline.
      2. reorganize.
      3. change the appearance.

5. Read lines 38–40.

    Pioneers are people who

    a. create new systems of government.

    b. set things up based on what they do not want.

    c. do something that no one has ever done before.

6. Read lines 45–47 "Many people were concerned that **power would fall into the wrong hands**…." This phrase means that

    a. the wrong person could gain power.

    b. the right person would gain power.

    c. many people would lose their power.

7. Read lines 50–54.

    a. What is a **dilemma**?

        1. It is a problem with two possible good solutions.

        2. It is a problem with two difficulties and one good solution.

        3. It is a problem with two possible solutions, neither of which is perfect.

    b. What follows **on the one hand** and **on the other hand**?

        1. The two possible solutions to the problem

        2. Two good solutions to the problem

        3. Two bad solutions to the problem

    c. What is the **heart and soul of the Constitution**?

    _____

8. Read lines 59–61. **In the hands of** means

    a. under law.

    b. under the control of.

    c. in the opinion of.

9. Read lines 64–65. **Hand in hand** means

    a. separately.

    b. carefully.

    c. together.

10. Read lines 77–85.

    a. What is a **bill**?

    _____

    b. Where did you look for this information?

    _____

c. This type of information is called
   1. an index.
   2. a footnote.
   3. a preface.
d. What does **veto** mean?

   _____

e. **Regardless of** means
   1. in addition to.
   2. because of.
   3. in spite of.
f. Complete the following sentence:
   Thomas wanted to go to the beach with his friends. The weather prediction was for rain in the afternoon. He decided to go to the beach regardless of
   1. the weather report.
   2. his friends.

11. Read lines 88–93. To **enforce a law** means to
   a. agree to a law.
   b. make sure a law is obeyed.
   c. punish people who disobey a law.

12. Read lines 94–96. They are **in safe hands** means the rights of the people are
   a. in danger.
   b. protected.
   c. important.

13. Read lines 97–99.
   a. Who was Thomas Jefferson?

   _____

   b. Where did you find this information?

   _____

   c. A synonym for **liberty** is

   _____ .

   d. When people are **vigilant**, they
   1. pay money for something.
   2. are alert to any danger.
   3. write their concerns on paper.

14. What is the main idea of the passage?
  a. American colonists fought a revolution to gain independence from Great Britain.
  b. American colonists created a new government that had a president instead of a king.
  c. American colonists gained their independence and created a constitutional government to ensure that no part of the government would have too much power.

Vocabulary Skills

PART 1

Recognizing Word Forms

In English, verbs can change to nouns in several ways. Some verbs become nouns by adding the suffix -*ment*, for example, *equip (v.)*, *equipment (n.)*.

Read each sentence. Complete each sentence with the correct word form on the left. Use the correct form of the verb in either the affirmative or negative. All the nouns are singular.

replace *(v.)*   **1.** The Continental Congress _____ the colonial government

replacement *(n.)*   when the colonies became independent. The _____ of the

previous government was an important first step.

pay *(v.)*   **2.** The Continental Congress _____ any people or

payment *(n.)*   countries it owed money to because it had no money of its own. The

_____ of an army or navy was impossible, too.

enforce *(v.)*   **3.** The _____ of the law is the job of the judicial branch of the

enforcement *(n.)*   government. It _____ all laws that have been agreed on by

the president and the Congress.

establish *(v.)*   **4.** The new states _____ republics and elected governors

establishment *(n.)*   for each state. The _____ of an overall government was a

difficult task.

agree *(v.)*

agreement *(n.)*

5. If the president _____ with a bill, he vetoes it. However, a bill can still become a law with the _____ of a majority vote in Congress.

PART 2

Understanding Collocations

Collocations refer to words that are often used together. They can help you when you write and speak. The noun *hand* is used in many different collocations, for example, *on the one hand*, *on the other hand*, *in the hands of*, *hand in hand*, *in safe hands*, and *fall into the wrong hands*.

First, match each collocation with the correct meaning. Then complete each sentence with the correct collocation. Use each collocation only once.

_____ 1. fall into the wrong hands   a. the first of two possible solutions to a problem

_____ 2. hand in hand   b. have the wrong person gain specific information or power

_____ 3. in safe hands   c. protected

_____ 4. on the one hand   d. the second of two possible solutions to a problem

_____ 5. on the other hand   e. in the care of someone

_____ 6. in the hands of   f. together

1. Liz and John just got married. They want to take a vacation, but they are not sure if they should. _____, they really enjoy traveling, but

_____, they need to save their money to buy a home.

2. When Sam became ill, he put his health _____ his doctor. Sam knew that she would help him recover quickly.

3. I don't carry my passport with me unless I'm traveling. I'm afraid that if I lose it, it will

_____ .

4. A nutritious diet and daily exercise go _____ for good health.

5. My mother takes care of my son when I am in class. I know that he is

_____ when he is with his grandmother.

Vocabulary in Context

Read the following sentences. Complete each sentence with the correct word or phrase from the box. Use each word or phrase only once.

dilemma *(n.)*	established *(v.)*	regardless of	therefore *(adv.)*
discontent *(n.)*	foundation *(n.)*	reluctant *(adj.)*	vigilant *(adj.)*
enforce *(v.)*	initial *(adj.)*		

1. Carlos was very unhappy with his job. Because of his _____, he decided to look for a new place to work.

2. The city _____ this university 75 years ago. Since that time, it has become a very popular college.

3. Fernando wants to become a doctor. _____, he will begin medical school in the fall to achieve his goal.

4. I was _____ to buy a new computer because of the high cost. However, when my old computer stopped working, I had no choice.

5. Zoe runs two miles every morning, _____ the weather. She even runs when it snows!

6. Do not drive over the speed limit. The police strictly _____ the law and will give you a speeding ticket if you drive faster than the limit.

7. My sister is always _____ when she rides her bike. She watches the cars and buses carefully to be sure she is safe.

8. An understanding of English grammar is the _____ for writing a good composition.

9. My friend invited me to a concert tonight, but I already have tickets for a basketball game.

    I'm not sure what to do. This is quite a _____ for me!

10. When Sandy first arrived in the new city, her _____ idea was that the people were unfriendly. However, she changed her mind after she made some new friends in just a few weeks.

Reading Skill

Using Headings to Create an Outline

Readings often have headings that introduce new ideas, topics, or details. Using heading to make an outline can help you understand and remember the most important information from a reading.

Read the article again. Underline the headings. Then scan the article and complete the following outline, using the headings that you have underlined to help you. You will use this outline later to answer specific questions about the article.

    I. The Origin of the Federal System of Government

        A. _____

        B. The Continental Congress existed, but had no legal power.

        C. Legal governments in the states were established to replace colonial rule.

        D. _____

  II. _____

        A. Its purpose was: _____

        B. The feelings of the writers of the Constitution

            1. _____

            2. They did not want a strong central government.

            3. _____

            4. _____

  III. _____

        A. The purpose of this system was:

            1. _____

            2. _____

            3. _____

B. The powers not given to the government belong to the states.

C. _____

IV. _____

A. The legislature, or Congress, drafts a law.

B. _____

C. _____

   1. _____

   2. If the president vetoes the bill, Congress can pass it anyway with a two-thirds majority vote.

D. If someone challenges the law, the judicial branch determines whether the law is constitutional or not.

Information Recall

Read each question carefully. Use the outline to answer the questions. Do not refer back to the text.

1. a. What kind of government did the United States have before the Constitution was written?

   _____

   b. Was this government successful? Why or why not?

   _____

2. What features of government didn't the writers of the Constitution want?

   _____

3. a. What is the purpose of the system of checks and balances?

   _____

   b. How does it work?

   _____

4. How are laws made in the United States?

_____

_____

_____

_____

Writing a Summary

A summary is a short paragraph that provides the most important information in a reading. It usually does not include details, just main ideas. When you write a summary, it is important to use your own words and not copy directly from the reading.

Write a brief summary of the passage. It should not be more than five sentences. Use your own words. Be sure to indent the first line.

Topics for Discussion and Writing

1. Alone or with classmates from your country, write a description of the form of government in your country. Compare it with the form of government in the United States. For example, how are laws made? Who is the leader of the country? How is he or she granted this position? Compare your country's form of government with those of the other students' countries.

2. The author states: "A government ought to have three major powers: to make laws, to carry out those laws, and to provide justice under law for the best interests of the people." Do you agree or disagree with this statement? That is, do you think these should be the major powers of any government? Explain your answer.

3. Write in your journal. Read the description of the system of checks and balances in lines 55–65. Do you think that this system adequately protects the people's rights and that it prevents the federal government from becoming too powerful? Explain your answer.

4. **Jigsaw Reading:** You are going to read about the three branches of the U.S. government: the legislative branch, the executive branch, and the judicial branch.

   a. First, read the paragraph entitled *The System of Checks and Balances* on page 220. Discuss it in class to make sure everyone understands it.

   b. Second, work in a group of three or four students. Each group will read about one branch of government on the following pages. Group A will read about the legislative branch, Group B will read about the executive branch, and Group C will read about the judicial branch. After reading the paragraph, discuss it to make sure everyone in the group understands about their particular branch.

   c. Third, set up different groups so that each group has a student or students who have read about the three different branches. In these new groups, tell each other what you have read about each branch. Take notes about the other two readings. Do not look back at your readings. Ask each other questions to make sure that all the students in your group understand how the three branches work.

   d. Finally, work together to complete the Federal System of Government Chart on page 224. When your group is finished, compare your chart with the other groups' charts.

The System of Checks and Balances

The writers of the Constitution wanted to make sure that the people's rights would always be safe and that the federal government would never become too powerful. Therefore, the writers of the Constitution set up three branches of government: the legislature, or Congress, to make laws; the executive branch—the president—to carry out the laws; the judicial branch, to watch over the rights of the people. The system of checks and balances makes sure that one branch cannot become stronger than another. This system not only balances power among the three branches but also provides a check on each branch by the others.

The United States Supreme Court and the Capitol dome

Group A Only: The Legislative Branch

The legislative branch, or Congress, represents all states fairly. It consists of two parts: the House of Representatives and the Senate. The vice president of the United States acts as the president of the Senate. Each state has two senators, who are elected every six years. The number of members in the House of Representatives[1] depends on the population of each state. Representatives are elected every two years. To be elected as a senator, a person must be at least 30 years old, have been a citizen for nine years, and be a resident of the state he or she will represent. To be elected as a representative, a person must be at least 25 years old, have been a citizen for seven years, and be a resident of the state he or she will represent.

The major job of Congress is to make laws. If the president vetoes, or rejects, a proposed law, Congress can pass the law anyway by getting a two-thirds majority vote. Congress can also declare war by getting a two-thirds majority vote of the senators and representatives. The House of Representatives can also impeach the president. This means that the House can charge the president with a crime. In this case, the Senate will put the president on trial, so the vice president must resign as the president of the Senate. The Senate votes to approve the justices that the president appoints to the Supreme Court. These are just a few of the legislative branch's many responsibilities.

Group B's Information:

_____

_____

_____

_____

_____

_____

Group C's Information:

_____

_____

_____

_____

_____

_____

_____

---

[1] The **House of Representatives** has 435 members.

Group B Only: The Executive Branch

The executive branch of the government puts the country's laws into effect. The president of the United States is a member of the executive branch. The president must be at least 35 years old and be a natural citizen of the United States. In addition, he or she must have lived in the United States for at least 14 years and be a civilian. The president is elected every four years and cannot serve more than two terms in a row. The vice president acts as president of the Senate. When the president receives a bill from Congress, he or she must sign it in order for it to become a law. However, if he or she disagrees with the law, he or she can veto, or reject, it. The president can also ask Congress to declare war. He or she also appoints the justices to the Supreme Court. He or she must do his job according to the Constitution, or he or she may be impeached, that is, charged with a crime by Congress. The executive branch is a very important part of the U.S. government and must work with the other two branches according to the Constitution.

Group A's Information:

_____

_____

_____

_____

_____

Group C's Information:

_____

_____

_____

_____

_____

Group C Only: The Judicial Branch

The judicial branch of government is the system of courts in the United States. Its job is to enforce the laws. The Supreme Court is the highest court in the country. It consists of nine justices: one chief justice and eight associate justices. The Constitution does not state any specific requirements for Supreme Court positions. The president appoints the justices, but the Senate must approve them. The justices are appointed for life. The Supreme Court not only makes sure that people obey the laws but can also declare a law unconstitutional. In other words, the Supreme Court can decide if a law is not in agreement with the Constitution. Furthermore, the chief justice acts as president of the Senate if there is an impeachment trial. In an impeachment trial, Congress charges the president of the United States with a crime. The judicial branch works together with the legislative and executive branches to protect the Constitution and the rights of the people.

Group A's Information:

_____

_____

_____

_____

_____

Group B's Information:

_____

_____

_____

_____

_____

In your groups, work together to complete the following chart using the notes that you wrote. Do not look back at the paragraphs you have read.

THE FEDERAL SYSTEM OF GOVERNMENT			
	Legislative Branch	**Executive Branch**	**Judicial Branch**
Function			
Number of Members	Congress: _____ Senators _____ Representatives	___1___ President _____ Vice President (acts as president of the Senate)	Justices: ___1___ Chief Justice _____ Associate Justices
Term of Office	Senators: Representatives:	President:	Justices:
Requirements	Senator: 1. at least 30 years old 2. 3. Representative: 1. at least 25 years old 2. 3.	President: 1. at least 35 years old 2. 3. 4.	
Responsibilities: Laws	1. 2.	President: 1. 2. 3.	
Responsibilities: War		President:	not mentioned
Impeachment	House of Representatives: Senate:	President: Vice President:	Chief Justice of the Supreme Court:

Critical Thinking

1. Read the first paragraph. Why does the article begin with a series of questions? In other words, what do you think is the author's purpose in asking the reader questions at the beginning of the reading passage?

2. Read lines 41–52. Why do you think these people were so sure about what kind of government they did *not* want?

3. After reading this selection, specifically lines 10–12, 15–17, 42–45, and 67–69, what can you understand about the individuality of the states in the United States? For instance, how do you think that the fact that the United States consists of 50 separate states affects American culture and the attitudes of the people in each state?

4. Read the last paragraph of the passage. What is the author's opinion of the U.S. system of government? How does the author feel about U.S. citizens' responsibility for making sure their rights are protected?

The United States Supreme Court

Crossword Puzzle

Review the words in the box below. Then read the clues on the next page. Write the words in the correct spaces in the puzzle.

balances	discontent	liberty	reshape
bill	domination	majority	therefore
cause	enforced	pioneers	veto
convention	foundation	regardless	vigilant
dilemma	initial	reluctantly	

Crossword Puzzle Clues

ACROSS CLUES

5. A federal law must be _____ in every state in the United States.

7. Many people _____ accepted a federal government. They really wanted each state to be mostly independent of the others.

10. Americans must be _____, or forever watchful, to ensure that they keep their freedom.

12. There was much _____ with the Articles of Confederation because the government did not have important powers such as borrowing money.

14. The American colonists successfully fought to overcome British _____, or rule.

15. The system of checks and _____ ensures that no one in government has too much power.

17. A bill can become a law _____ of a president's veto with a two-thirds vote in Congress.

18. The Constitution is the _____, or basis, of the American system of government.

DOWN CLUES

1. Each state wanted to maintain its independence. _____, the original form of government was very weak.

2. The men who created the federal system of government were truly _____. This was a completely new form of government.

3. The president has the power to _____ a bill by refusing to sign it.

4. The U.S. Constitution was written to _____ the government because the Articles of Confederation did not work well.

6. A(n) _____ is a meeting that a group of people hold in order to make decisions.

8. _____ is another word for "freedom."

9. A(n) _____ is a proposal for a law.

11. After declaring independence, the _____ step was to establish governments in every state.

13. A(n) _____ consists of more than half (at least 51 percent) of a group.

14. A(n) _____ is a problem with no perfect solution.

16. The colonists fought hard for their _____. They wanted independence from Britain.

INDEX OF KEY WORDS AND PHRASES

Words with **AWL** beside them are on the Academic Word List (AWL), Coxhead (2000). The AWL is a list of the 570 highest-frequency academic word families that regularly appear in academic texts. The list was compiled by researcher Avril Coxhead from a corpus of 3.5 million words.

SKILLS INDEX

CRITICAL THINKING AND DISCUSSING

INTERNET

READING

TOPICS

VISUAL LITERACY

Completing charts, 55, 87, 224
Creating:
    flowcharts, 52
    information charts, 163, 198
    outlines, 33–34, 142–143, 160–161, 216–217
    outlines from headings, 160–161, 180–181, 216–217
Crossword puzzles, 20–21, 38–39, 56–57, 74–75, 90–91, 108–109, 128–129, 146–147, 164–165, 184–185, 202–203, 226–227
Understanding:
    charts and graphs, 16–17, 40, 124–125
    graphics, 122–123
    timelines, 71, 201
Using a Venn diagram, 104–105

VOCABULARY, GRAMMAR, AND USAGE

Dictionary use: 31–32, 102–103
Recognizing word forms:
    noun and verb forms that are the same, 68, 195
    suffix -al, 12–13, 101–102
    suffixes -ance and -ence, 30
    suffixes -ion or -tion, 49, 120, 177–178
    suffix -ful, 157
    suffix -ity, 84–85
    suffix -ly, 139
    suffix -ment, 213–214
Understanding:
    antonyms, 13–14
    collocations, 214
    meaning in context, 14–15, 32–33, 51, 70, 86–87, 103–104, 122, 141, 159, 179–180, 197, 215
    phrasal verbs, 69, 85–86
    synonyms, 50, 140, 158, 178–179
    useful phrases, 196
Using common expressions and idioms, 121
Word meanings, 9–12, 26–29, 44–48, 64–67, 81–84, 97–101, 116–119, 135–138, 153–156, 173–177, 191–194, 208–213

WRITING

Journal writing, 19, 36, 55, 72, 89, 106, 127, 144, 163, 183, 200, 219
Recalling information: 18, 36, 53, 54, 72, 88–89, 106, 126, 144, 162, 182, 200, 218
Topics for writing, 19, 36, 55, 72, 89, 106, 127, 144, 163–164, 183, 200, 219
Writing a summary, 18, 36, 53, 72, 88–89, 106, 126, 144, 162, 182, 200, 218

CREDITS

NOTES

NOTES

NOTES

NOTES

NOTES

NOTES

NOTES

NOTES

NOTES